HONOLULU HOMICIDE

MURDER AND MAYHEM IN PARADISE

Gary A. Dias and Robbie Dingeman

Illustrations by Gayle Taketa

3565 Harding Ave.
Honolulu, Hawai'i 96816
Phone: (800) 910-2377
Fax: (808) 732-3627
www.besspress.com

Design: Carol Colbath

Dias, Gary.
  Honolulu homicide : murder and mayhem
in paradise/ Gary A. Dias and Robbie Dingeman ;
illustrated by Gayle Taketa.
      p. cm.
  Includes illustrations.
  ISBN 1-57306-156-5
  1. Police - Hawaii - Honolulu -
History. 2. Criminal investigation -
Hawaii - Honolulu - Case studies.
3. Crime - Hawaii - Honolulu -
Case studies. 4. Homicide
investigation - Hawaii - Honolulu.
I. Dingeman, Robbie. II. Taketa,
Gayle, ill. III. Title.
HV7911.D52.A3   352.2-dc21

Printed in the United States of America

For

Ryan, Kevin, Samantha, and Alexis,
because they make everything worthwhile,

and

the rest of our families, our mothers, auntie, brothers, sisters
and our friends who encourage and support us in so many ways,
and our late fathers, who helped guide us along the way

Any man's death diminishes me, because I am involved in mankind;
And therefore never send to know for whom the bell tolls;
It tolls for thee.

—John Donne

Contents

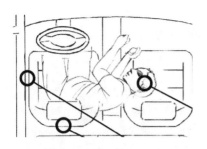

Workplace Violence

Police Officers as Victims and Perpetrators

Puzzles

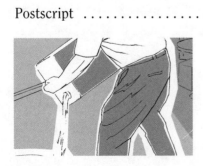

Acknowledgments

We would like to thank our daughters for putting up with us as we spent long nights putting words to paper. The "Mommy, are you done yet?" and "Daddy, not another book!" comments gave way to quiet reading time and sleep as the evenings progressed. For their eventual understanding (and leaving us alone while we worked) we are grateful.

A note of thanks is also owed to the Honolulu Police Department for their assistance in providing the mug photographs used in this book. And more broadly, we wish to thank the people and the organizations that helped shape our careers, expertise, and opinions: again HPD, for Gary. For Robbie, *The Honolulu Advertiser* (her day job, which keeps her honest), and previously the *Honolulu Star-Bulletin* and KHON *Channel 2 News*.

We also wish to thank and acknowledge Gayle Taketa, of Charles Taketa Graphic Design, Inc., who developed and drew the illustrations used in this book. Her art was essential in depicting some key points throughout the text where photographs were not possible.

We would like to offer our sincere thanks to Lorna Kanehira for her frank and loving discussion of her late husband, Ford Kanehira.

And we must thank each other for taking part in this risky venture, working together on a project despite some very different views on certain subjects. People warned us of the dangers of building a house together. Well, they should try writing a book. Wrestling with the emotional topic of serious crimes that dramatically affect others can be draining and ultimately a sad reminder of some very bad times for so many. But the whole experience has also been a reminder of the shared values and interests that brought us together in the first place.

Preface

Honolulu Homicide draws on the most notorious years of Gary's police career, his six years as the lieutenant in charge of the Honolulu Police Department's homicide detail. It also draws on other major crimes that occurred in Honolulu during the 1980s and 1990s.

The homicide job presented a unique opportunity to work with a small but very talented group of investigators in a team that saw the most horrifying things one person can do to others. As the years have passed, people have continued to ask Gary about many of the crimes we discuss in this book, wanting to know more, wanting to know what really happened.

As a reporter—then covering the police beat for *Channel 2 News*—Robbie was present at many of the homicide crime scenes described in this book. Her insight into investigations from a reporter's perspective adds a dimension to these stories that few see. In addition, through her reporter assignments she has had the opportunity to interview victims' families and conduct sometimes extensive research into victimology—the background and history of the victim. She covered some of the stories early in her career with the *Honolulu Star-Bulletin* and others more recently as she continues her work as a reporter with *The Honolulu Advertiser*. Her newspaper work is particularly evident in her knowledge of Honolulu's serial killings of the 1980s and the disappearance of Diane Suzuki. Although we both contributed to the book, for simplicity it is presented from Gary's perspective except for the closing chapter.

Lots of people ask us, "How did you two meet?" It was strictly business, and people get the strictly business answer. The actual answer was provided by a friend who kidded Robbie when she heard that we were engaged: "I just knew you met over some dead body." People usually laugh politely when we repeat that and wait for the true answer. But that's it. Not literally of course, but we did meet at a murder scene. Deputy Police Chief Warren Ferreira paged Gary at the scene of a double murder at 2211 Ala Wai Boulevard in Waikīkī.

The investigating team had been at the crime scene for about seven hours. Ferreira said the reporters were complaining that their deadlines were coming up and they hadn't gotten any information. He told Gary to go downstairs and brief the reporters and photographers waiting on the sidewalk; one of them was Robbie. The conversation with the reporters went something like this:

Reporters: Can you tell us what happened?

Dias: We have a double homicide.

Reporters: Tell us about the murders.

Dias: Two men are dead."

Reporters: How did they die?

Dias: They were killed.

Reporters: What killed them?

Dias: I can't tell you at this time.

Reporters: What can you tell us about the men?

Dias: We believe at least one of them lived here.

Reporters: What else can you tell us about the men?

Dias: We cannot say anything until families are notified.

Reporters: Is there anything you *can* tell us?

Dias: No.

After waiting outside for seven hours and paging the deputy police chief to get information from the homicide lieutenant at the scene, the reporters were less than thrilled with that exchange. (Since then, the interaction between police and reporters has improved, thanks to Chief Michael Nakamura's policy of openness with the community.)

Weeks later, we were more formally introduced by Nestor Garcia, who worked with Robbie at *Channel Two News* at the time. She was replacing Garcia as the police reporter. Because one of us was a police officer and the other a reporter, it took years for us to get to know each other. In fact, that first conversation amounted to us both agreeing that we had jobs to do and that we should lay out ground rules. Robbie told Gary that she understood that he would likely not give her all the information she wanted, but she couldn't abide people lying to her. As we all know, the police don't lie. But as Lord Tyrell of England said long ago, referring to government officers speaking to the media, "You think we lie to you. But we don't lie, really we don't. However, when you discover that, you make an even greater error. You think we tell you the truth." What he meant was that there are times that the police will not be able to discuss all the information obtained from a crime scene, particularly a homicide.

In this book, we have tried to give readers a behind-the-scenes look at the work involved in the investigation of murder and other serious crimes. We have also tried to preserve the dignity of the victims and their families while accurately describing the circumstances of their deaths. And we have walked the tightrope of telling the story without revealing information that would hamper police or prosecutors from ever taking some of the unsolved crimes to trial. Where conversations are quoted, we obviously don't remember the exact words spoken by everyone. Rather, the quotations reflect the feeling and gist of the conversations as we remember them. In the Kāhala Panty Burglar case, the names of the victims were changed to protect their identities.

We focus on more recent events that more closely touched our lives—cases that inspired great work, cases that have been solved and that remain unsolved. We explore some of the methods, procedures, and techniques involved in the investigation of major crimes, including forensic science, a topic of great interest in communities across the nation. And we provide our opinions on various law enforcement issues, opinions that to some may appear too idealistic, or critical of current practices.

This is not a complete account of every homicide that occurred during Gary's homicide assignment. That does not mean that other cases, not mentioned here, are less important. Rather, we chose a sampling of cases that drew and held the community's interest and concern or that were representative of the many other investigations. In several chapters, we discuss cases in which people were not murdered, but which generated widespread community interest, such as the Kāhala Panty Burglar case and the Stan Cook shooting.

Another focus of this book is the dedication that the men and women of law enforcement across the nation must have when they devote their lives to the investigation of murder. It is a grisly field of work that requires an intense devotion to doing things right. It is a field of work that changes those who undertake it. It affects our view of the world, and we must guard against developing a perception that humankind is basically evil. It is a profession that causes us always to be on guard. To watch for criminal activity. To watch for people who are irrational because of the crystal methamphetamine they use. It changes our lifestyle. We become overly cautious with our children (and our spouses) and we worry when they go off to routine activities such as school excursions and birthday parties.

So we find that distant spot in our souls where we put our fears, and we wear a normal face, and we approach our work with a façade that seems cold, uncaring, and emotionless to others. We have to, or we become like the detective at the murder scene of a little girl who was the same age as his own daughter. He weeps and grieves for that innocent child, and in his grief, he risks missing crucial evidence.

In this book we also focus on the old Hawaiian concept of *kīnā'ole,* as taught at the Queen's Medical Center by the late George Kanahele.

Kīnā'ole means you
> *do the right thing, in the right way, at the right time,*
> *in the right place, to the right person, for the right reason,*
> *with the right feeling—the first time.*

We'll show, in the stories that follow, just how important it is to do the right thing when investigating homicide investigations.

Introduction

People have asked me, "What's it like to investigate a homicide?" The answer is complex. Yes, the process includes specific steps and procedures, but it also includes principles, ideals, and beliefs. Probably the best way to explain it is to take you there, to describe in detail a case, to put you in the investigators' shoes. It starts like this:

Standing in the doorway of the old house in Pearl City, I could feel the history of the family who lived there: fading graduation pictures rested on the valance above the wooden venetian blinds, geisha dolls stood in old glass boxes on shelves alongside the TV, and an array of family portraits were arranged on one wall. The house was single-wall construction, made of redwood, and bordered Moanalua Road in Pearl City. The carport had long been without a car; boxes and stored goods took over the available parking space.

Sitting on a rusted metal-frame chair in the carport was an old man. He was dabbing at his tearful eyes with a kitchen towel as he occasionally looked up at the young uniformed officer standing next to him.

"Who would do this to her?" he asked, not able to fathom that his wife of fifty years lay dead in the hallway with a pillowcase tied tightly around her neck.

As I stood looking at the body of the elderly woman, my patience was tested by the young night-shift detective who had been sent to preserve the scene and await the arrival of the homicide detectives.

"Geez, what the hell do you do first?" he asked in wonder.

It was tempting to make some wisecrack like "Isn't it great when crime-scene investigators don't know what to do first," but I held my tongue. Six years earlier, I had been in his shoes, and it didn't seem right to criticize him for expressing what we'd all felt at some point. Years later, I would understand that the police department itself created the young man's indecision, by expecting a new detective to complete accurate investigations from the start. Instead, the bureaucracy should have recognized that new detectives are very much like recruit school graduates: they understand the process, but they don't have the experience.

A lecturer at a homicide seminar I attended at the New York State Police Academy described three characteristics that are of utmost importance to a homicide investigation: organization, thoroughness, and caution.

Organization. Being unprepared and disorganized can defeat an investigation. "What the hell do you do first?" is an unacceptable question for a detective to ask at a homicide investigation. Understanding not only the first steps, but the entire process will affect the investigative outcome and will reflect, either favorably or poorly, on the professionalism of the investigator and his or her efforts to process that murder scene.

Thoroughness. When was the last time you went to work and deliberately decided to do a half-assed job? This characteristic—thoroughness—is perhaps the most important of the three. When you break down the crime-scene tape, send the patrol officers back to their beats, and drive away from that crime scene, you're saying that you're done. Thoroughness applies not only to the crime scene, but also to the processing of evidence back at the station, to the follow-up witness interviews, and subsequent suspect interrogation. Failure to do these things thoroughly can have disastrous effects.

In the late 1980s, an eight-year-old girl in San Diego was raped and sodomized. The investigation focused on her father as the suspect, even though she told police and social workers that a stranger broke into her room and took her out the window. She was taken from her family, and her father was subsequently arrested and charged with the offense. For two years, a semen stain on the girl's nightgown went undetected by detectives, police evidence specialists, and criminalists. Then DNA testing of the stain proved that the father did not rape his daughter. The father's defense team found a suspect who had committed similar rapes in the vicinity of the girl's home. Further testing found that the suspect was indeed the rapist. The lack of initial thoroughness in this case proved to be a nightmare for the girl's father, but more important, think of the severe psychological damage inflicted on this young victim by the state, the police, the prosecutors, and the social workers, who insisted that her father raped her, when all along she knew otherwise. All of them were responsible to the victim and her family to conduct the best possible investigation: the most well organized investigation and the most thorough investigation. And yet they failed.

Another consequence of an incomplete investigation is the destruction in court of a detective's credibility as an investigator.

"Detective," asks the defense attorney, "did you perform this very important procedure in the course of your investigation?"

"No," answers the chagrined detective, who must be honest, in spite of the embarrassment.

Then comes the dreaded question, the one he absolutely knows will follow.

"Why not?"

There's no acceptable answer to the "why not?" when a detective fails to follow basic investigative procedures or forgets something. The jury won't forget. And more important, neither will the judge, who may look at him with a wary eye during all future cases.

Caution. To step lightly. To understand techniques and procedures. To protect any aspect of the investigation from contamination. Perhaps these are the easiest to do because we are taught the rules of the investigative process. Unless, of course, we get lazy and fail to follow the rules we set for ourselves, or the rules set for us by science or the courts.

"Excuse me, Lieutenant, I'm going to check the floor for any evidence." The evidence specialist slowly entered the house in Pearl City to search the floor for any obvious and maybe not-so-obvious items of evidence that would tie the old woman's killer to the scene. And then the evidence specialist would work to recover this evidence before the major investigative effort began. The woman's body would not be approached again until all evidence around her had been identified and recovered. I say "again" because the very nature of this work involves contamination by people who have already been to her body, those who first found her and tried to see if they could help her before determining she was dead. These people included the husband who found her, the uniformed officers who first responded to the call for help, the paramedics who gave medical information to doctors via a telephone for her death pronouncement. But now that she had been pronounced dead, the preservation of the crime scene became the important task at hand.

Crime scene preservation has a two-part definition. *To keep the crime scene in the same condition in which it was left by the perpetrator* is the first, and easy, part. This is important because the scene will talk to us. I didn't originate this phrase or concept. I remember hearing an investigator at a homicide seminar discuss just *how* a crime scene will speak, and *what* it will say. With the help of our eyes, our experience, and our common sense, the scene will tell us what happened. With the help of our knowledge, the scene will help us reconstruct what occurred. It will *talk to* us. And we must let it talk to us before we go charging into the scene; otherwise, we may miss some very important information.

The second part of the definition of crime-scene preservation is *to prevent the adding or taking away of any items that may be evidence.* This can be difficult to accomplish, because, in most cases, by the time the first officer arrives at a crime scene, someone has already contaminated it. "Contamination" is not a bad word here. It's merely descriptive. Officers and other people entering a crime scene—the family, police, emergency crews—contaminate it. But *adding* or *taking away* items of evidence? Who in his right mind would do that? Anyone who walks into the scene. We bring things into the scene on the bottom of our shoes and take things away in the same manner. We shed hair. We shed clothing fibers, too. Each of these can be mistaken for evidence that was present prior to our arrival, and must be collected . . . and must be sorted . . . and must be compared. Lots of work only to discover that the hair was left by someone other than the killer.

More serious is the fact that we inadvertently contaminate the scene by leaving our fingerprints. This happens when an officer is concentrating so much on what he has to do that he accidentally touches something.

Can you remember everything you touched an hour ago? Maybe a few things. A minute ago? Sure. Now add in the conditions of responding to a murder crime scene, seeing the body of the victim, perhaps the bloody body of the victim. First, you check the scene to ensure the culprit is not still there, because you're no help to the victim if you end up dying alongside him. You check the body for signs of life, and your mind races as you wonder what to do next, who to call for help, and perhaps you may not remember what you touched—a minute ago.

We do things automatically. We turn on the light switch in a darkened room. Could the killer's fingerprints have been there? In checking a body for signs of life, we may need to assume an off-balance position. Without thinking, we may reach out our hands to touch or hold something to keep ourselves from falling. And we leave our fingerprints at that location at the scene. Most of the time, we don't intentionally contaminate a crime scene.

Except in the murder case of state Representative Roland Kotani. A ranking police official deliberately removed an item from the scene out of a misguided sense of loyalty to his boss. That executive officer actually took Kotani's driver's license from a pile of credit cards lying on the living room floor. He told us later that he took the license to show the identity of the victim to his district major. (I guess he thought his major wouldn't believe him without photographic proof.)

Inadvertent contamination is one thing. It can even be acknowledged in some cases as a good-faith effort by the officer to do what is right or necessary at that moment. Deliberately removing an item from a crime scene like a scavenging tourist is inexcusable. A good cop is an inquisitive cop, but one who knows limits and uses caution in investigative procedures.

However, limits should not apply when determining the boundaries of a crime scene. The killer leaves evidence long before entering and long after exiting the scene. The crime scene should be defined to include not only the location where the crime occurred, but also any possible avenue of the attacker's approach or escape. Officers sometimes find footprints or shoe prints outside the crime scene. Or tire prints that may link a killer's vehicle to the scene. Or an item of evidence that was dropped accidentally. On the street outside Michael and Wendy Touchette's residence in Kailua, where Orlando Ganal killed two of the Touchette children in an arsonist's blaze, Ganal accidentally dropped a shell casing that he used in Waipahu to kill his in-laws an hour earlier. This shell casing proved to be a critical piece of evidence that linked Ganal to the killings at both scenes.

Locating and identifying evidence is one of the important tasks at a crime scene. But we can't go about this task haphazardly. There must be some reason to our efforts. A good rule of thumb is that the processing of a crime scene occurs from the outside in and from the ground up. This rule allows us to recover evidence we may otherwise be stepping on as we go about our business. One underlying truth in homicide cases is that we usually don't know what happened. *We simply don't know.* The key witness is dead. Therefore, we must process and investigate the scene as if any and every possibility exists. The biggest flaw a homicide investigator can exhibit is to *assume* that the activities between killer and victim occurred in a certain and specific manner and sequence. This closed view can easily overlook what really occurred, leaving the investigation with false leads.

Sometimes it is easy to develop opinions that fit a preconceived notion, particularly when there is an easy person to target. When this occurs, the investigator may be driven solely to find evidence to prove that one person's guilt. In this case, investigators should remember that *evidence is anything that can prove guilt or inno-cence, provided it can be presented legally.* Guilt *or* innocence. The police must never forget that it is equally their responsibility to prove innocence as it is to show guilt. And if the police cannot present evidence legally at trial, it's not evidence. In fact, the court will not accept evidence that was obtained in violation of the Fourth Amendment.

In the various college courses Gary teaches on law enforcement, he stresses the Fourth Amendment as the legal foundation police officers must commit to memory and refer to every time they investigate a crime. If you're having difficulty recalling the Fourth Amendment from your high school American Government class, here it is:

The right of the people to be secure in their persons, houses, papers, and effects, against unreasonable searches and seizures, shall not be violated, and no warrants shall issue, but upon probable cause, supported by oath or affirmation, and particularly describing the place to be searched, and the persons or things to be seized.

The concept of being secure against unreasonable search and seizures came about in the 1700s as the result of the English practice of issuing a Writ of Assistance, which allowed the British to enter colonists' homes searching for untaxed goods. It seems that the British in the Colonies at that time didn't follow their own beliefs that a man's home is his castle.

In the eighteenth century, around the time of the American Revolution, British statesman William Pitt said in his speech on a British excise bill:

The poorest man may in his cottage bid defiance to all the forces of the Crown. It may be frail; its roof may shake; the wind may blow through it; the storms may enter, the rain may enter, but the King of England cannot enter; all his forces dare not cross the threshold of the ruined tenement!

Simply put, a man (or woman) must be secure in the freedom of his person, of his home, of his papers, and of his goods against unreasonable searches and seizures. British statesmen before the American Revolution believed in this, the framers of the United States Constitution believed in this, and we must believe in this today.

Sam Dalton, a long-time public defender in New Orleans, spoke the ultimate truth about our Constitutional rights in a *Listening To America* television special titled "And Justice for All." Dalton said,

The Bill of Rights is the only thing the common people have. It's the only thing that separates us from power, and it's the only thing that tells government it's gotta behave. And every time we don't exercise those rights, or we don't protect them, we shorten the length of time that those rights are going to survive.

In the same program, New Orleans Judge Calvin Johnson said, "We have to create in the minds of individuals the perception that this is a system that works for everyone, no matter color, no matter class, but it works for everyone." When we investigate a murder, or any other crime for that matter, we must know, understand, and protect the Fourth Amendment rights afforded all of us.

The crime scene of the Pearl City woman's murder was considered a simple one. Reconstruction suggested that a burglar entered the home. The woman surprised him and he killed her. The evidence was straightforward. The processing of the building was not difficult. The troublesome issue was that someone's wife, someone's mother, and someone's grandmother lost her life because a petty thief panicked. It was now our job to find the answer to her husband's sad and tearful question: "Who would do this to her?"

1
The Murder of Roland Kotani—Part One

On July 28, 1989, I got a call from my captain about what I knew would be a high-profile homicide in Pearl City. The victim was State Representative Roland Kotani. My mind swam with the consequences of such a case. My first thought was that there would be intense interest from the media, as well as from government officials. I also thought back to the murder of Senator Larry Kuriyama in ʻAiea many years before, and how difficult that case was to solve.

Kotani's body was discovered that morning, after he failed to report to his office and no one answered telephone calls to his residence. The quiet Leeward neighborhood was buzzing with onlookers and news media when investigators arrived. The scene itself, though, was quiet—all the people who had been inside the house earlier were now outside waiting for the Homicide Detail and Evidence Specialist Team to assemble and begin the long process of identifying and gathering evidence.

One of the first concerns my bosses passed on to me was that we *really* needed to solve this case. In fact, I was told that money was not an issue here—that the governor had offered money to the city to help with the investigation. I never spoke to the governor about the case, so I don't know if that was true or not. I just knew that a high-profile person had been brutally murdered, and we had been charged with finding his killer. I did have the cynical thought that, *Sure, money is no object here, but it certainly was for the last murders we investigated*—*"watch your overtime."* But I've learned to leave the personal thoughts and cynicism behind and concentrate on working the crime scene and discovering as much evidence as possible that may lead to the killer. In Kotani's case, the evidence began right inside the front door.

Kotani's house had a strange setup. The front door was hidden from the street by the carport. The door opened into the living room immediately adjacent to a set of sliding glass doors that also opened into the living room. Those sliding doors were ajar, while the front door was closed and locked. In a small pile on the living-room floor were loose credit cards and other items normally found inside a man's wallet. One key item was missing, however—the driver's license. At the time, we didn't know what to make of this, so we gathered up the wallet and its spilled contents and moved on. We would learn later that the driver's license was removed from the wallet by the overeager ranking administrative officer described in the Introduction. Enough said about him.

Music records and tapes were strewn about the floor. In the kitchen, cabinets and drawers were open. The refrigerator door was ajar, and a milk carton was on the counter. A few food items were scattered on the floor. A burglary? More likely, the killer had tried to make the house *look like* the scene of a burglary. All the homicide detectives at Kotani's crime scene were at one time or another burglary investigators. They all agreed this case did not have the look of a burglary.

In Kotani's bedroom, the drawers to his dresser and nightstand were pulled open and a few items strewn on the bed. For several reasons, we were certain these staged searches were performed quickly after the killing: Kotani was not killed instantly with the first blow. He made an effort to escape or fight off his attacker. The assault traversed the bedroom. Perhaps Kotani called out for help. The assault itself—a banging against walls, the impact of the weapon against Kotani's head—probably made a lot of noise. Neighbors might have called the police. It made no sense for the killer to remain in the house searching for a few items of value after committing a violent murder. Kotani was the target.

And motives we got, from many sources. Too many motives. Gambling. Women. Drugs. Politics. Yes, politics. One TV reporter stated that he had *reliable* information that Kotani, a Democrat, was murdered by other Democrats who suspected him of masterminding a campaign smear against former congressman Cec Heftel. Heftel believed that he lost to John Waihee in his bid to become governor because of that smear. These suggestions of various possible motives offer a perfect example of the reason police officers and detectives must keep their minds open to all possibilities.

Normally, a crime-scene investigation works from the outside in and from the ground up to avoid disturbing unseen evidence. So in this case we moved cautiously from the outside of the house inward, clearing a path toward the body in the master bedroom, realizing that other personnel—initial HPD officers and Emergency Medical Services paramedics—were there ahead of us. As much as we want to protect the crime scene from contamination, it's not possible. The first officers on site need to secure the scene from further danger. They may need to offer first aid. The emergency medical team must concentrate their efforts to save a life if possible. Saving a life will always take precedence over evidence. Often it's too late, and the paramedics' task is to determine that the victim is truly dead.

In this case, it was obvious Kotani was dead. He was lying on his side against the wall near the foot of his bed, his head and shoulders resting in a large pool of drying blood. From the doorway of his bedroom, we could see that post mortem lividity had already begun; gravity was pulling his blood to the lowest points of his body. Rigor mortis—the stiffening of the muscles after death—was also in effect. The smell of the decaying blood filled the room and told us he had died hours before. The injuries to his head indicated that he had been killed with a blunt instrument. It wasn't until the medical examiner's investigator moved him that we got a better look and saw injuries typically associated with blows from a hammer.

The wall behind Kotani was spattered with his blood. The blood spatter showed different characteristics, from droplets to swipes and smears. This evidence provided important clues in our reconstruction of the offense. With then-Captain Wilson Sullivan leading the Evidence Specialist crime scene team, we photographed, diagrammed, studied, and conducted an analysis of the bloodstain pattern.

At the same time we were conducting the bloodstain pattern analysis, we learned some critical information. Kotani, thirty-five at the time of his murder, had been in the legislature for two years, representing the Pearl City-Pacific Palisades area. He was well liked, and people thought he had a bright career in government ahead of him. A magna cum laude graduate of Yale University and a student activist at the University of Hawai'i while earning his master's degree, he had a reputation as someone who was open-minded and stood up for what he believed in. When the move to make Martin Luther King, Jr.'s birthday a state holiday was being debated, most of the backers were a core of liberals, many of them African-American, who diligently pushed for the holiday. Sometimes they testified, and sometimes they wrote letters, but they also marched around the state capitol courtyard to call attention to their cause. And right in the middle of those quiet marchers was Kotani, trudging along to support the effort, without purposefully calling attention to himself.

His personal life lacked that clarity and direction. He and his wife, Grace, were married for nearly ten years and had a three-year-old daughter. However, they had been separated since February 1989. His friends told us he had recently broken up with a girlfriend.

Kotani's personal life interested us because his death scene showed many signs of overkill. He had many blows to his head and face—many more than were necessary to kill him. He was beaten while he was on the bed, alongside the bed, at the foot of the bed. He was beaten while he was standing, kneeling, and lying down. Burglars don't commit overkill. "Hit men" don't commit overkill. Overkill is, however, common among lovers or people with emotional attachments to each other, as well as in hate crimes, in which a victim is chosen because of his race, religion, gender, disability, or sexual orientation. There was rage associated with Kotani's murder, a rage that a burglar or a hit man wouldn't have.

The bloodstain pattern analysis enabled us to reconstruct the sequence of events. Sheet and bedcover positioning indicated that he was lying on the right side of the bed when he was first assaulted. We know this initial assault didn't kill him. The final position of his body and the massive bloodstain pattern on the walls told us much more.

The murder scene of Roland Kotani

Following the clues offered by the blood droplets, we concluded that he awoke with the first blow and rolled toward his left to attempt escape. He climbed out of the bed—probably more awake now, but confused and in great pain. The blood spatter on the curtains and file cabinet next to the bed showed that as he stood on the left side of the bed his assailant continued to strike him with the hammer. We suspected his assailant pursued him across the bed and continued to strike him from above while standing on the bed over him. Still attempting to flee, Kotani then moved toward the foot of the bed, his killer following him and continuing to strike him on the head. The bloodstain pattern showed that Kotani, bleeding heavily and dazed from his wounds, stopped fleeing at this point. His head fell back against the wall, evidenced by a circular smear made by his blood-saturated hair. He collapsed to his knees, his head leaving a six-inch-wide swath of blood as he fell, sliding down the wall. We know he didn't fall directly to the floor, because there on the wall, at about his kneeling height, was the bloody impression of the side of his left arm, the curve of the side of his palm, and the three segments of his fifth finger. We envisioned him reaching out his arm to steady himself after he fell to his knees, using the wall for support. But it would be fruitless. The bloodstain pattern showed that the assault continued while he knelt, the hammer blows striking his head from the right and from the left. The blood droplets indicated the hammer was swung both downward and from side to side. How could we tell? Cast-off blood spatter—blood that had clung to the hammer and was cast off as the hammer was quickly pulled back by the assailant before delivering another blow—appeared on both sides of the body. At some point, Kotani fell to the floor. But the assault didn't stop. Blood spatter also indicated that he was struck while he was lying on his side.

By the time the killer stopped hitting him, Kotani was either dead or near death. The scene was literally a bloody mess. But a most curious fact existed. There was not one drop of blood outside Kotani's bedroom. Not one. The amount of blood on the walls and floor indicated that the assailant would be covered with blood and would have stepped into blood. The killer's hands would be stained with blood, and the weapon would be dripping blood. Yet not a trace of blood was found in the rest of the house. Why were there no blood drops on the floor? Why were there no bloody footprints or shoe prints leading from the murder scene? It would be a few days before we knew the answer.

We used all crime-scene investigative techniques available to us during this investigation, including a laser and fluorescent dusting powder. The laser provided a high-intensity light beam, and the fluorescent dusting powder would highlight any latent, or hidden, fingerprints found by the laser. The problem was that the laser's beam was only about three inches in diameter, and we were going to use it on every surface that the suspect may have touched, from above head height to the floor, throughout the entire house. The underlying principle behind the intense crime-scene work is simple. As we pointed out in the Introduction, we really don't know what happened. We really don't know what the suspect touched. We weren't there. So we don't assume. We accept the tedious nature of this business when we accept the responsibility for finding the killer of a human being.

Two decades ago, a good police investigation consisted of photographs, diagrams, and interviews. If we managed to get a confession, we scored. Today, we can't depend on a confession to get a conviction. Trials have become sophisticated events forcing the police to change the way they look at crime scenes. Defense attorneys have become more and more successful at getting their clients off the hook, requiring police and prosecutors to rely more heavily on science to prove their cases. The investigators' tools now include lasers, chemicals, and scanning electron microscopes. Cameras, pencils, and grid paper are still used, of course, but crime scene investigations have benefited from the sophistication of forensic science.

Microbiologist and forensic science author Kenneth Raines defines "forensic science" as the body of tested knowledge obtained through the scientific method and used in a court of law to discover the truth. Jim Wiese, a British Columbia science teacher and author of kids' science books, offers a kid-friendly explanation. He says "Forensic science is the study of objects that relate to a crime. These objects are called evidence. Forensic scientists study evidence so that it can be used as proof in court. The term forensic means "suitable for a court of law."

Of course both definitions are correct. I had a teacher at the FBI academy who gave an even simpler definition: science as it relates to law enforcement. Whichever definition you choose, it must be understood that criminal investigation is based partly on science, partly on good communication skills, partly on good observation, and partly on determination and thoroughness, not to mention an occasional good dose of luck.

When crime-scene investigators pore over a murder scene, they use different fields of science to identify and gather evidence: physics, chemistry, math, and biology to name a few. They also call for help to some crime scenes, bringing in scientists from various fields to assist with the investigation. These scientists include forensic odontologists (who are dental experts), forensic entomologists (who study insects), forensic profilers (who prepare a psychological/personality profile of the suspect based on the evidence), and forensic pathologists (doctors who conduct autopsies to determine cause of death).

In processing homicide crime scenes, evidence specialists perform a series of important, standard tasks. To document the crime scene, they take a series of photographs. It's not uncommon for evidence specialists to take two to three hundred photos at a murder crime scene: photos of the neighborhood where the crime occurred; location photos of the general, immediate scene, including the street fronting the house and the exterior of the house itself; the interior of the house, showing general details; and close-up photos, to highlight any item of importance. The difference between close-up photos and evidence photos is that an evidence photograph includes a ruler to provide scale.

In addition to photos, diagrams are prepared. Diagrams and photographs not only document the scene but also convey to the judge and jury exactly what the scene was like at the time of the investigation. The most common type of diagram is the floor plan diagram, also known as the "blueprint" or "bird's eye" diagram. Other types of diagrams are the elevation diagram and the exploded view, the latter a combination of the floor plan and the elevation diagram. In murder cases, the diagram is drawn to scale; that is, every $1/4$ inch equals 1 foot. Creating murder diagrams is tedious. The measured distances of the scene's walls, doors, and windows must be included, and every important item or piece of evidence must be accurately placed in the diagram through triangulation (measuring a cross-point from two perpendicular walls).

After all evidence items are located, photographed, and diagrammed, they are recovered, placed in paper envelopes or bags, and secured until they can be submitted to the Evidence Room. This aspect of the crime-scene investigation is what got the Los Angeles Police Department's evidence specialists into trouble when O. J. Simpson was on trial for murder. An evidence specialist placed an item of evidence into his shirt pocket while conducting other crime-scene business, in violation of policy and procedures. Simpson's defense attorneys were successful in alleging that evidence was mishandled and created doubt regarding that evidence specialist's professional integrity.

The next important procedure is the processing of the victim's body. Very little is done at the crime scene. The body is photographed and its position on the floor recorded in the diagrams. Any obvious evidence on the body that could be lost during transport is recovered at the scene, but otherwise the body is processed in more detail at the morgue.

The primary evidence we were looking for during that early stage of the Kotani investigation was fingerprints. Even with the advances made in DNA technology, fingerprints remain the best type of evidence we can ask for. Fingerprints form in the embryo stage and remain unchanged through death. Three types of fingerprints can be recovered from a scene: plastic prints, or prints left in puttylike material; prints contaminated with a foreign matter such as blood or paint; and latent prints, formed when oils on fingers are transferred to a surface.

There are many ways to develop fingerprints at crime scenes. The most common method uses fingerprint powder to obtain prints from smooth surfaces. For prints on paper, a common technique uses a liquid ninhydrin solution. When the paper is treated with the solution, it reacts with the amino acids of the print, turning the print purple. Another method of print development, accidentally discovered by a scientist in Japan, is superglue fuming, which produces a white print on nonporous objects. Whatever the process, the search for fingerprints at a murder scene remains perhaps the most critical aspect of the investigation.

While the evidence specialists investigated the crime scene, the detectives spoke with coworkers and neighbors, trying to get as much information as they could concerning Kotani's life and associations. In our preliminary discussions, we considered the possibility that Kotani was murdered by the girlfriend he recently broke up with, since their break-up allegedly went badly, and since the killer possibly had an emotional attachment to Kotani.

The crime-scene investigation and preliminary interviews took several days. The first formal interview we set up was with Kotani's estranged wife, Grace. We hoped she would be able to provide us with personal information about Roland Kotani that we didn't get in the preliminary interviews. Her interview was scheduled in the evening at the Criminal Investigation Division of the Honolulu Police Department's headquarters on Beretania Street at Pāwaʻa Annex.

Grace Imura-Kotani arrived for the interview on time and was taken to the Homicide Detail's office in the basement. She was dressed in jeans and a blouse and she carried a purse. I offered my condolences for the death of her husband and asked if she would like some coffee. I also inquired if she had eaten dinner. She smiled and politely declined the offers of food and drink. We understood that this was probably a very difficult time for her and we didn't want to prolong it any further, so detectives took her to our interview room a few feet down the hall from the Homicide Detail office.

The interview room was a small, plain office with a small, square table and straight-backed metal office chairs with padded seats and backrests. The room was designed to eliminate distractions, and all interviews in the room were recorded, on both audiotape and video-tape.

The lead detective began the interview. He thanked Grace for agreeing to meet with us and offered his condolences. Grace nodded. And then she said the words that set off the sequence of that night's astonishing and tragic events:

"I killed my husband."

The detectives were taken aback, and didn't immediately believe her. Occasionally someone takes responsibility for the death of another because of something else they did or did not do. In this case, one of the detectives told me later that he thought she might have still been in shock and felt responsible for Kotani's death because their marriage failed—had their marriage been successful, he would still be alive. But she repeated her claim that she was the murderer. There was one way to know for certain. Only the investigative team and the killer knew that the murder weapon was a hammer. We had kept this information to ourselves. We had also kept to ourselves all descriptions of evidence and our suspicions regarding the reconstruction of the crime. It's a common investigative practice. With this information, we can weed out false claims. We can also verify a suspect's confession. We asked Grace Kotani, "How did you kill your husband?"

"I killed him with a hammer."

2
The Murder of Roland Kotani—Part Two

Her response was calm and deliberate: "I killed him with a hammer."
Grace never flinched. She spoke clearly, and her emotional and
physical behavior seemed normal. Too normal. When the detectives
overcame their initial shock at her sudden confession, they notified
me and continued to interview her. When a murder suspect confesses,
we need to be absolutely sure that the person confessing is the true
killer.

A groundbreaking case in England illustrates one way of identifying a false confession. In 1985, Dr. Alec J. Jeffreys of Leicester
University in England developed the DNA testing that we use today
in criminal cases. He also coined the term "DNA fingerprints." His
method of DNA examination was first put to the test in 1986, when a
young man confessed to and was charged for one of two rape-murders
that seemed to be committed by the same person. DNA testing dis-
proved the claim.

A more common way to test a confession is by asking the confessing person to describe in detail what happened during the crime.
In Roland Kotani's case, we had developed a sequence of events that
told us what happened from the moment the first blow was struck.
We could compare Grace's account with our detailed reconstruction.

Grace began by describing the events that occurred before the
murder. She told the detectives that she and Roland were separated,
but she had always hoped they would reconcile, even though she
knew he was seeing another woman. The day before the murder, she
went to the house with their daughter on a scheduled visit. They all
gathered under the tree in the yard. Roland seemed relaxed and
happy. They were sitting on lawn chairs while the little girl played.

Grace said she got up and walked behind Roland and put her arms around him, giving him a hug. She felt the moment was right and wanted to show him that she believed they could get back together. But he did something that froze her heart and set the wheels in motion for his death.

"He grabbed my hands and pulled them off of him and pushed me away," she said. "He told me not to touch him, that he didn't love me anymore. It was at that moment that I knew I was going to kill him. I just knew I was going to kill him, and that I had to do it very soon."

Grace recalled that after Roland pushed her away, she became quiet and began to think of how she was going to kill him. After the visit, she took their daughter to a relative's house and went to a hardware store and bought a hammer.

She prepared everything she would need to commit the murder. Then she waited. She waited for the dead of night, and then drove to Roland's house. After parking her car a few houses away, she walked to her former home and into the yard behind the carport. The doors were locked, but—moving silently—she used her key to get in.

"I wanted to make it look like someone broke into the house and killed him."

She said that she locked the front door again, but unlocked and opened the sliding glass doors in an effort to show that a burglary had occurred. Then taking the hammer from a plastic bag, she walked down the hall to Kotani's bedroom.

"He was sleeping. I stood over him for a minute. Then I raised the hammer and hit him on the head. He jerked and made a sound, moving away from me. I hit him again. He was awake now and he went across the bed and stood up. I climbed up onto the bed and followed him. I stood on the bed over him and hit him again and again while he was standing next to the window. He staggered a few feet toward the bathroom. I got down from the bed and hit him again. He made a long, drawn-out grunting—groaning—noise. I stood in front of him and hit him again and again. He fell to his knees and I kept hitting him. When he dropped to the floor, I thought he was dead, but then I heard him breathing heavy, so I continued to hit him as he lay there."

Grace recounted the scene with the demeanor of someone detailing a familiar recipe, sounding as if she were discussing a normal activity that she had recently completed. The detectives needed more detail.

"How did you hold the hammer?"

"I held it with both hands," described Grace, bringing her hands together as if she were holding a baseball bat.

"And how did you hit him? Did you hit him using the same motion, like someone would in hitting a nail?"

"No, I swung the hammer from both sides, hitting him on the sides of his head, on the top of his head. I think I hit him in the face a few times."

Grace's description of how she hit him, where in the room the attack took place, and where on his body she inflicted his injuries all fit our reconstruction of the murder. The pattern of the blood spatter told us that the blows were coming from all directions. This suggested that the killer was swinging the hammer from side to side. We discussed this fact at the scene and agreed that it was quite possible the killer was a woman holding the hammer with both hands because she lacked the strength to use one hand. A man who used a hammer to kill someone would probably hit the victim with much more force than we saw in Kotani's case. He would also be likely to use the hammer exactly as if he were striking a nail, using his stronger hand and arm to deliver but a few fatal blows to the same part of the victim's head. In our assessment of Kotani's injuries prior to autopsy, we saw injuries that barely broke skin and some that broke bones in his skull, but none that suggested the hammer burst through his skull and into his brain.

The element of rage suggested by our reconstruction was also proved by Grace's statement. The multiple injuries to Kotani showed that the killer's state of mind was intentional and that the intent was to injure again and again, culminating in the murder of the victim.

To be very angry at someone and strike out at them is one thing. But to continue to attack, to follow and corner the victim as you maintain an incessant assault, to carry through your actions even when you see the injuries and pain you are causing, all tell of an uncontrollable rage. In Kotani's case, even as he lay dead or dying on the floor, Grace's rage was so great that she continued to slam the hammer into his head.

Grace's admission and detailed description meant that we now knew for certain who the killer was. Further questioning told us more about her state of mind.

"Do you know if he recognized you? Did he say anything?"

"He didn't say anything. He only grunted a few times. One time was a long, drawn-out groan. I don't know if he recognized me."

"Why did you use a hammer?"

"I wanted to hurt him."

The detectives told me later that they were astonished at her frank, cold statement that she wanted to hurt him. A frank statement, yes, but it spoke of the rage that she had toward him. Although Grace was consumed by rage, she still plotted Roland's murder with precise calculation.

"What happened after you killed Roland?" she was asked.

"I opened some drawers in the bedroom to make it look like a burglary. I knew there would be a lot of blood, so I wore a clean set of clothes under the bloodstained ones I was wearing. I took off my bloody clothes and put them into a plastic bag along with the hammer before I left the bedroom. Then I went into the living room and did a few other things to make it seem like he was killed by a burglar."

"What did you do with the plastic bag?"

"I threw it into the garbage can at the curb as I left. It was garbage collection day, and I knew the hammer and bloody clothes would be long gone by the time someone found his body."

This was more evidence that Grace's actions were calculated and deliberate. Her efforts to plan the murder, to commit the crime in the dead of night to hide her identify, and to destroy or eliminate evidence were characteristic of a person who understood that what she was doing was wrong. Why she admitted so readily to committing murder remains unknown.

The detectives completed their preliminary interview and informed me of her statements. My next task was to call the commander of the Criminal Investigation Division (CID). He was excited that we were able to conclude the investigation so quickly. The department's administration would be happy, the governor would be happy, the legislature would be happy, and he was happy.

Grace came out of the interview room with the detectives for a break and sat in our office. Once again we offered her food and coffee. We had not yet placed her under arrest because we wanted to talk with her more. We were afraid that if we arrested her, she might realize how serious the situation was and stop talking to us. So we decided to wait until we were completely finished with the interrogation before formally arresting her. She did have one request as she rested in our office.

"I need to go to the bathroom," she said. "I'm having my period and I need to change my pad."

Her utter frankness to three strange men was startling. Of course we would allow her to go to the bathroom; however, we would accompany her. I instructed one of the detectives to take custody of her purse and accompany her to the women's restroom in the hallway just outside CID.

I was sitting at my desk a few minutes after they left my office when I heard a muffled "boom" through the walls of the building. I instantly recognized the sound, but thought that yet another police officer's gun had gone off in the locker room, and I hoped no one was injured. Seconds later I heard running footsteps coming down the empty CID hall, followed by someone shouting, "Lieutenant! Lieutenant!" I recognized the voice as one of my two detectives. "She shot herself! She shot herself in the bathroom!"

I was stunned. The detective turned and started running back to the women's bathroom. I ran after him. My mind was whirling. When we reached the restroom, the detective whom I earlier assigned to carry her purse was standing next to the door looking devastated.

"What happened?" I asked.

The detective looked on the brink of tears.

"We got to the door and she asked for her purse. I told her I had to hang onto it, and she said again she needed to change her pad and that she had another in her bag. She opened the purse and took out a sanitary napkin bag. And then she went right into the bathroom. A second later we heard a gunshot. I'm sorry."

At the moment I didn't know what to say. I pushed open the door and walked in. Grace was lying on the floor with her head to the far wall and her feet near the stall's door. Her legs were apart slightly, and lying between her legs was the gun she used to kill herself. It was partially wrapped in a red bandanna. On top of the toilet paper dispenser lay a white paper sanitary napkin bag. Grace's head lay in a pool of dark blood. Flowing away from her body, the blood lightened in color until it was a clear pink liquid—a sign that spinal fluid was escaping. There was no sign of life.

The ambulance had already been called, and we were waiting for the paramedics. I looked closer at her head. There appeared to be a cruciate wound to the right side—evidence that when she pulled the trigger, the muzzle of the gun was in contact with her skin. When a gun is placed to the skin of the head and fired, the gases follow the bullet into the wound and some of the gas is forced between the skin and bone of the skull, forcing the skin away from the bone. This tears the skin into a star-shaped, or cruciate, wound.

I looked around the stall and saw an impact crater in the concrete to the left of her body. On the opposite side of the stall lay the deformed bullet, hair and bits of flesh still clinging to it. I looked again at Grace. In spite of the violence of her death, she looked at peace. But I felt myself getting very angry. I was angry that we failed to prevent her death. I was angry because I knew there would be difficult questions to answer. I was angry at Grace because her suicide did not bring closure to the murder; it would only open the investigation to intense questioning. Another person was dead, leaving a little girl without either parent. We had felt victory at Grace's confession; now we were engulfed in a sense of failure.

The paramedics arrived, and within a minute, after transmitting the information to a doctor, they pronounced Grace dead. It was difficult for the brain and soul to accept. Minutes earlier we were speaking to a breathing, thinking, feeling human being. Then in an instant, her act of self-destruction left us with a body and many unanswered questions.

Questions about our procedures came up in the review by the department's administration. Did we do the right thing by allowing her to go to the bathroom? Why wasn't she arrested, so she could be searched before she went to the bathroom? Why didn't we have a female officer accompany her into the bathroom? In hindsight, we could have done a number of things differently. The fact remains that we acted on what we decided was the best course of action at that moment.

The department's administration themselves made an error in a news release to the media. Obviously, Grace's confession to her husband's murder, then her planned suicide, created a media frenzy unlike any I've seen before or since. The media demanded as much information as possible, so a news release was scheduled. All the facts were given to the media at this news release, including a description of the weapon Grace used to kill herself. Big mistake.

Grace killed herself with a .357 magnum. Just the name alone implies a gun as big as a cannon. After telling the media that Grace used a .357 magnum in her suicide, the department officials promptly refused to discuss it further or to allow the media to see the weapon. And rightly so. We didn't need to set a precedent of allowing the media to view evidence. So the next thing a good reporter would do is go straight to a gun dealer and ask to see a .357 magnum. And what would any respectable gun dealer do? Show them the biggest and shiniest .357 magnum he had in stock. So on the evening news, Honolulu looked at a .357 magnum with what appeared to be a 12-inch barrel—in other words, a cannon. And then some of the media suggested that the police were lying to the public because how in the world could Grace Kotani hide such a large gun in her purse? How could a trained detective miss such a weapon?

One reporter caught me in the hall with the TV camera rolling, in what is called an "ambush" interview. "What are you hiding from the community in the Grace Kotani death? Was her death really a suicide, or was she murdered? Did the police murder Grace Kotani?"

The reporter was trying to get a knee-jerk reaction from me. I guess she was hoping to get me on videotape ranting and raving at her ludicrous questions. What she got was a pretty disgusted cop who refused to answer her questions and who left her standing in the hall. She didn't make it into the division. Her video didn't make it to the evening news either.

The reality is that the .357 magnum used by Grace was a snub-nosed revolver with a two-inch barrel that—even when wrapped in the bandanna—fit nicely into the disposable sanitary napkin bag. Her weapon was slightly larger than a snub-nosed .38-caliber revolver. It was not the cannon portrayed by the media. The gun, bandanna, and bag were photographed and documented as part of the official record of Grace's suicide. We satisfied the requirements of the investigation, but apparently not the overworked imaginations of several reporters.

The bottom line in the deaths of Roland Kotani and Grace Imura-Kotani was simple after all. Grace murdered her husband out of the rage and hatred she felt toward him because of their failed marriage and personal relationship; then she killed herself. Some later theorized that it should have been obvious that someone of Japanese ancestry would have been planning her suicide from the start. While it's clear that there is a cultural history of ritualistic suicide in Japanese culture, it wasn't obvious that this modern Japanese-American woman would take this action. The cultural theory would require her to murder her daughter, not orphan her. It's insulting to Japanese-Americans and the investigators to assume that her actions would be dictated solely by the culture of her ancestors. It's also much easier to second-guess someone's motives when you already know the outcome—when you haven't been working for many hours under intense scrutiny, when it's not the middle of the night, when you don't have to tell this woman who has spent hours unburdening her soul, "Sorry, no, you can't go to the bathroom unless you let me search your feminine hygiene products."

It has been suggested by some that she killed herself out of shame for murdering her husband. Others have suggested that she killed herself because she knew she would eventually be caught and that she didn't want to go to prison. One thing is certain. She gave no indication that she planned to kill herself and offered no signal to the detectives that she was about to take such a violent action.

As she did with the murder of Roland Kotani, Grace Imura-Kotani planned her suicide with cold, calculating precision. She decided what she was going to do, prepared for it by hiding the weapon in her purse, feigned a need to be alone in a clever way that she must have known few men would question, then committed the act of suicide at her first moment of opportunity.

Grace and Roland would both later be described as wonderful, caring people with bright days ahead of them.

Except for those two tragic nights in the summer of 1989.

3
The Murder of Marialyse Catell

I recently got a telephone call from a nurse manager at The Queen's Medical Center, where I work as the manager of security, asking for advice. She said that one of her staff nurses was having trouble with her husband. She moved out of the house, and the soon-to-be ex-husband threatened to kill her. Because he had beaten her in the past, she was afraid that he would actually try to kill her, so she obtained a temporary restraining order (TRO) from the court to prohibit her husband from coming near her at her home or place of work. "Is there anything we can do about this?" asked her manager.

My memory went back to two murder cases in which the victims, Junko Whiting and Lynn Kotis, had taken out TROs against their violent husbands:

On Thanksgiving Day in 1991, Timothy Whiting walked into the Sheraton Moana Surfrider Hotel where his wife Junko worked. He went straight to his wife's department, walked past fellow workers, and stabbed his wife to death. He then calmly walked out. He made no effort to hide who he was from her fellow workers, who knew him and knew that Junko had taken out a TRO against him.

Timothy Whiting was charged with murder in the second degree. The jury disagreed with the charge and convicted Whiting of manslaughter; they thought he was under extreme emotional distress at the time of the murder.

The second case was similar in that the marriage of Lynn Kotis and William Kotis, like that of Junko and Timothy Whiting, was breaking up. Lynn left William and, because of previous abuse, she obtained a TRO against him. Lynn moved to Waikīkī and tried to get her life back in order. She met a man named Gregory Whittman and began dating again.

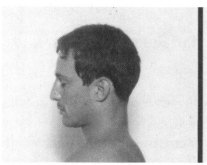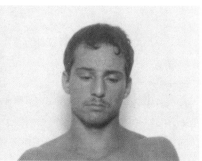

The mug photograph of William Kotis

William, however, wanted to get back with Lynn. His obsession grew, and one day he decided that the only way to be with Lynn again was to kill her and then commit suicide. Or so he claimed. On September 7, 1992, he waited in the parking lot of her apartment, armed with a hunting knife and a shotgun. When she arrived with Whittman, he confronted them with the knife and tried to drag Lynn into his car. Whittman intervened, and William pulled a shotgun out of the back seat. Lynn and Whittman backed against a wall, which Whittman climbed. Lynn begged William not to hurt her and even offered to leave with him. William, however, shot her at point-blank range. Lynn fell to the ground and William shot her again and again. An off-duty police officer who was passing by attempted to stop William, who was fleeing, and shot him in the buttocks.

How did I answer the question asked by the Queen's nurse manager? I told her that she should be alert to the possibility that the woman's husband could come onto the Queen's campus. She and the staff should know what he looks like and call security if he shows up. Frankly, I believe TROs don't work in cases in which the violent person is determined to hurt the victim.

Perhaps our legislators will one day come up with a law that will put some teeth into TROs—before more women like Junko Whiting and Lynn Kotis die.

Not everyone who kills a spouse or lover is a man. Not every murder involves obvious extreme emotional distress. And not every case has a complex motive.

The homicide team was called to a house on the Wai'anae Coast early one morning to investigate the stabbing death of a man. When we arrived, we met with a woman who claimed she accidentally stabbed her boyfriend.

She said she was standing at the kitchen counter, slicing a block of Spam on a cutting board, when her boyfriend snuck up behind her and tickled her ribs. She said she was so startled by the sudden move that she jumped and jerked her arms above her head. Unfortunately, the sharp knife was still in her hand and she accidentally stabbed her boyfriend in the neck. He stumbled around the kitchen, which was next to the living room, leaving blood spatter in various places before he collapsed and died.

Corroborating her story was the chunk of Spam still on the cutting board. The fact that she remained at the scene seemed to further support her story that the killing was an accident. One problem: the neighbors all said that the two fought constantly and that the woman frequently beat up her boyfriend.

We began our investigation by photographing and diagramming the scene. Then we analyzed the blood spatter on the floor and on the walls in an effort to reconstruct the victim's movements after he was stabbed. Something didn't fit. The blood spatter suggested he was running around not only the kitchen but also the living room before he collapsed, which contradicted her account.

As we continued to process the kitchen, one of the evidence specialists lifted the block of Spam and the sliced pieces lying next to it. We found blood underneath the Spam. This told us that the blood splattered onto the cutting board before the Spam was sliced and placed there. The woman was lying. She was also subsequently convicted of second-degree murder. One of the detectives dubbed it our first case of Spamicide. But he didn't say it to make light of the death. It was just such a strange case.

While this was a case of a woman murdering her male companion, men who kill their wives or girlfriends far outnumber women who kill their husbands or boyfriends. And not every case comes from a failed temporary restraining order.

On April 16, 1988, twenty-four-year-old Marialyse Catell was murdered by her husband Michael Catell. Marialyse's body was never found, and Michael has refused to tell anyone what he did with her body.

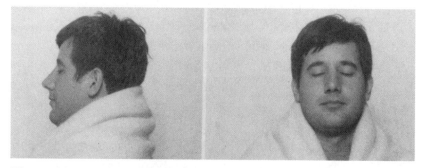

The mug photograph of Michael Catell

Marialyse and Michael were having marital problems. About a year before he murdered her, Michael suspected her of having an affair and becoming pregnant. On April 16, his rage exploded into violence. At about ten minutes after 5 A.M., neighbors heard a loud argument occurring in the upstairs portion of the Catells' apartment at 861 Ala Liliko'i Street in Salt Lake. Then they heard what sounded like someone beating another person. Shortly after that, they heard four to six gunshots. A few minutes later, they heard a loud bumping noise, as if something was being dragged down the stairs and hitting hard on each stair landing. The dragging continued outside, where neighbors saw Michael dragging what looked to be a military footlocker. He put the footlocker in the bed of his truck and drove off before the police could arrive. On the blood-covered bed in the master bedroom lay a three-month-old infant girl.

Michael worked for the navy, so naval police were notified to be on alert for his truck.

Evidence in the case indicated that Michael probably shot his wife and took her body somewhere to hide the murder. He subsequently turned himself into Pearl Harbor naval base police.

On April 17, 1988, the day after the murder, a footlocker was found at Pier 35 in Honolulu Harbor. The footlocker contained pools of blood. We suspected that it was the footlocker that Michael dragged through the house. In a careful examination of the home's carpet, we had found several tiny slivers of wood. When the footlocker was discovered, we found the precise locations on the footlocker where the wood slivers came off. The matches were nearly perfect. The slivers, which were of irregular shape, fit into the locations on the footlocker, helping to prove that it came from the house.

But the footlocker was not found until the day after the crime. This could have presented a difficulty later in court. Defense attorneys

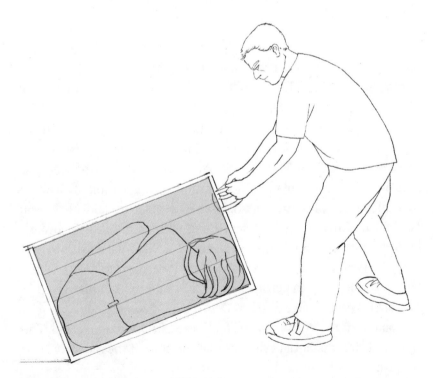

Michael Catell dragging off the footlocker

would ask, "Could someone have tampered with the evidence?" The answer would have to be yes.

Marialyse's body was missing. Could we prove that Michael killed his wife? The first thing we had to prove was that Marialyse was dead. Medical Examiner Mary Flynn was summoned to the scene. Several facts became important:

- Marialyse was a small woman who weighed less than one hundred pounds.

- Brain and bone tissue were found in the bedroom where the shooting occurred.

- The quantity of blood found in the bedroom and in the footlocker was estimated by Dr. Flynn to be between one and two liters.

After examining the quantity of blood, Dr. Flynn gave us her professional opinion. Based on the historical circumstances of the marital problems between Marialyse and Michael and of the factual information regarding Marialyse, Dr. Flynn concluded that a woman of Marialyse's size and weight, having lost between one and two liters of blood, would go into shock and without medical treatment would die.

Now to prove whose blood it was. The only reliable answer would come as the result of DNA testing. We received permission from the attorney general to obtain a blood sample from the infant. We also took blood samples from Marialyse's parents, Mr. and Mrs. John Ishmael of Guam. The samples, along with samples of blood and brain tissue from the scene, were sent to a mainland lab for DNA analysis. Within a few weeks, we had positive confirmation that the blood sample from the crime scene matched both samples given by Marialyse's parents. We also had DNA analyses conducted on samples of blood from the house and the footlocker. Those too matched. This was good circumstantial evidence that the body of the murdered person had been placed in the footlocker.

Although we didn't have her body, we now had proof that

Marialyse Catell was murdered on April 16, 1988. The statement from Dr. Flynn and the DNA analysis gave us a victim.

Our focus then became a search of various areas where Michael could have buried his wife's body, if indeed that was what he did. We spoke to people who knew him and asked if they knew of any spot on the island where he liked to go, any favorite hiking trail, park, beach, etc. There were few suggestions. So we concentrated on the open and secluded areas within a five-mile radius. We thought that Michael, suspecting that the police would be looking for his truck, wouldn't have driven very far. We searched open places, like parks. We used dogs, and officers used long slender metal rods to determine whether the soil had been loosened or upturned recently. We found no trace of Marialyse. Our not finding her angered her parents, who thought we should have been able to at least find her body. I completely understand their anger. Losing their daughter in such an unexpected, violent way must have broken their hearts.

Several months after Michael was charged with Marialyse's murder, an inmate from the prison where Michael was being held came forward and provided a statement that Michael told him he killed Marialyse because she was unfaithful—that it was simpler to kill her than go through a divorce. Michael told him that he took her body to a gravesite he had dug earlier and buried her. Michael bragged that he would be convicted of the lesser offense of manslaughter because he was under a lot of stress and that he would serve three or four years and then be paroled on good behavior.

Shortly before his trial, Michael's confidence was lagging a bit. His attorney announced that Michael would agree to show us where he buried his wife if we would allow him to plead to manslaughter. Apparently, he thought he might not win his case. The prosecuting attorney said "no deal," and Catell was found guilty of murder in the second degree.

We may never find Marialyse, but perhaps her family can rest easier knowing that her killer was convicted of her murder and sentenced to life in prison.

4

The Kāhala Panty Burglar—Part One

An increasingly frightening series of events took place in Honolulu in the early 1980s. It started with someone's fascination with women's underwear—a fetish—which is how the case got its nickname: the Kāhala Panty Burglar. In the beginning, the crimes were a curiosity, almost a joke.

I was assigned as the Burglary/Theft Detail detective for the Kāhala-to-'Āina Haina area. It was not an extraordinarily busy beat, but property crimes throughout the neighborhoods kept the police busy. When people think of Kāhala, they think of a rich neighborhood filled with mansions, luxury cars, and celebrities. But Kāhala is much more than that. It's an old area of Honolulu, where quaint beach homes, local-style family residences, and small cottages shoulder up alongside the stucco villas. Yes, there are millionaires living in Kāhala. But there are also middle-class folks—teachers, store clerks, students—and people starting out in their careers, some of whom live in the many cottages that dot the area.

One day we began to see minor thefts pop up at homes along Kāhala Avenue and the nearby streets: thefts of women's panties from their clotheslines. These thefts were obviously minor in terms of expense. (How much does a pair of panties cost? Back then, a couple of dollars?) At the time, the penal code described this level of theft as a misdemeanor. From the standpoint of the theft-division detectives, this type of theft was a nuisance. It fell into the realm of complaints from people irked by those who steal mangoes from a tree bordering a sidewalk, or newspapers from a front porch. The thief was probably some young kid or group of teenagers looking for cheap thrills in the neighborhood.

At the onset of these thefts, they never struck me or any of the other detectives in our detail as a big problem. We would smile and laugh at the cases as they came in, and joke to ourselves that "at least the panties were clean when they were stolen off the clotheslines." We were obligated to investigate these cases just as other detectives were obligated to investigate robberies and murders. But we had no evidence and no witnesses. This was the type of investigation we threw back to the patrol guys. We asked the beat officers who were meeting with the women making these complaints to please look in nearby garbage cans. Perhaps the kids were throwing the panties away. More likely, the panties were part of a double-dare challenge issued by other kids in the neighborhood.

But the beat officers didn't catch any kids in the act or find any stolen panties. I and the other sector detectives began studying fetish crimes. We didn't like what we learned: that such crimes usually develop into something more serious. Several months had passed since the first theft case, and we were no closer to solving these thefts. We still had no evidence, no witnesses, and no suspects. The victims were frustrated at our failure to catch whoever was causing them this headache. But since the escalation we feared never materialized, we relaxed a bit and started to accept the fact that some cases never get solved.

Soon, however, we began to see some disturbing similarities among the theft victims. They were all Caucasian women. They were young and pretty. And they all lived alone or with other young and pretty Caucasian women. We were now pretty certain that these thefts were committed not by a group of young kids, but by one person, someone who targeted pretty young Caucasian women.

Then it happened.

One woman reported that her home had been broken into while she was at work. Only one thing was found to be missing: her panties. Hers was only one of several burglaries that occurred in the Kāhala Avenue area over the next few weeks. Each of the victims found only panties missing. Immediately the detectives in our detail began to work together more closely to catch the crook. We shared leads on cases and helped each other with follow-up activities and strategies.

It stopped being funny. The crimes did escalate, mirroring what we had learned about fetish crimes. The thief had became a burglar. We now were looking at felony offenses. Even more distressing, the felony crimes had sexual undertones. We discussed the cases with the Sex Crimes Detail to see if related cases had occurred in other neighborhoods. We discussed the cases with the Kāhala beat officers. And we discussed the cases with our bosses. Our biggest fear now was what might happen next. We feared that the crimes would escalate from property crimes to violent crimes. We feared that someone would get hurt.

And escalate they did.

One morning we were assigned a burglary case with a new element. Up until then, the burglaries occurred while the women were at work. This case was different. The burglar entered the woman's home while she slept. This outraged and offended the victim. This also offended us. It meant that the burglar had taken the crime to a different level— a dangerous level, because this victim had been burglarized once before while she was at work. This time, the victim didn't realize that she had been burglarized again while she slept until she walked to her car and made a frightening discovery. Her gas tank cover was missing, exposing the pipe leading to her gas tank. There at the opening of the pipe were her panties—stuffed in and hanging from the pipe opening. She was shocked and terrorized by this discovery. The knowledge that someone had entered her house while she slept, stolen her panties, and perhaps even stood over her, watching her, violated her sense of security and left her feeling absolutely vulnerable.

We faced our own fears and concerns about the facts of the investigation for these burglary cases:

• The perpetrator had escalated in his crimes from minor thefts to felony burglaries.

- His initial distant and hidden offenses committed while the victims were away had turned into more risky and dangerous acts while the victims were asleep at home.

- His offenses, while classified with the penal code definitions of theft and burglary, were definitely sexual in nature.

- The sexual nature of the crimes was deviant. What he was doing affronted and offended society.

- The burglar's actions had changed and now seemed designed to intentionally terrorize the victim.

- The burglar knew the Kāhala area well enough to successfully elude capture.

Our bosses were becoming as concerned as we were. They wanted briefings to learn what we were doing to catch the person terrorizing the Kāhala community. We thought we were doing everything we possibly could with the resources available to us.

Then the level of terror went up again.

Lisa, a young woman who had been burglarized once before, became a victim a second time. This time, however, she received a telephone call. From the burglar. At first she thought it was a prank call from someone who just wanted to talk dirty to a woman. Then he told her things that chilled her through and through. He told her how he watched her sleep. He described what she wore as she slept. He told how he pulled her panties from her drawer. He described her bedroom in enough detail to convince her that he was actually there. Then he told her that the next time he went to her house, he would rape her.

Lisa asked us, "How did he get my telephone number?" We told her it wouldn't have been difficult. Take a quick look around your own home. Look at your bills lying on the counter or desk. If you're typical, your telephone number can be found in several places in your house.

The telephone call hit Lisa very hard. She decided the threat was too great, and she was frightened enough to leave Hawai'i and return to her hometown of Los Angeles. She was gone within a week.

Lisa's roommates were also terribly frightened, but since they were not targeted they decided to remain in the house. We stepped up patrols of the house and general area, but there were no further problems after Lisa left.

However, Lisa was gone for only about two months. During those two months, the fear she had of the Kāhala Panty Burglar grew fainter, and she missed Hawai'i. She missed her roommates and friends. She missed Waikīkī and the Kāhala beach she loved so much. So Lisa decided to come back. She returned to the cottage that she shared with friends and was even able to get her old room back. One of her old roommates met her at the airport and drove her home. It was a bright, sunny day with blue skies and a cool breeze. The first thing she did when they got back to the house was run to the back-yard and look at the beach. She remembered thinking that the ocean would be warm. She and her friend changed into their swimsuits and hit the water. After a long-awaited swim, Lisa lay on a towel on the sand and dried off in the sun. An hour later, she and her friend returned to the house. No sunburn for Lisa on her first day back. The telephone rang. Lisa answered the phone.

"Welcome back, Lisa. I've been waiting for you."

She was devastated. He was watching her. He was waiting for her. How could he know? How could he know the day of her return? How could he know that she was back? How could he know she was on the beach? She left Kāhala again, and that was the last we heard of her. We never learned if she just found a house away from Kāhala or if she returned to Los Angeles for good. But we knew one thing for sure that we hadn't known before. The burglar was in the area. He was watching. He was looking for his next victim. And he remembered his previous victims. We all thought that Lisa just happened along while he was there, watching. He remembered her. And he focused on her and waited for his opportunity to call.

Our panty burglar had taken his deviant sexual offenses to a higher level. In turn, our level of concern also rose. The frustration we felt grew, and we became even more focused and determined to identify him. Investigating these cases was no longer just our job. It became our mission.

The first thing we did was develop undercover stakeouts of the Kāhala area. We knew another victim lived across the canal that bordered Kāhala Beach Park. She had been burglarized by the panty burglar before, and we thought it was possible that he would strike again. We chose her as a potential victim, and we planned our stakeout of her house. We were cautious. If our stakeout was obvious, the suspect would be wise to us. On the other hand, we needed to have enough personnel to adequately respond if he struck. We hid officers in bushes of the houses next door to the potential victim. We had a "chase car" ready in case the suspect managed to get into a vehicle and flee. The victim knew of our efforts, cooperated fully, and appreciated knowing that police officers were just outside her house. The only other thing left to do was start the stakeout and wait. Had we chosen the right potential victim? Had we picked the right time for this stakeout? Had we trained our officers well enough to prevent burning our cover? We could only hope. Hope and wait and pray that he would burglarize this woman again.

We arrived early enough not to be obvious and simply sat out our time, waiting and watching. I was in the chase car with another officer, Allen, at the Kāhala Beach Park parking lot for a few nights. Allen was a trusted officer with really good street smarts. He was a good cop and he knew his business. He worked in the surrounding area and knew the neighborhood and people. I valued his opinion and I knew that with him on our team we had an edge.

The stakeout went on for days. Nights actually, because it was during the night that the panty burglar hit. It was on one of those long stakeout nights that we realized that pretty much anyone passing by us would know that we were police officers watching for something, simply by the way we behaved. We acted like cops on a stakeout. That wouldn't do. We needed something to make our presence there seem more normal. Beer. That would make us seem like a couple of normal guys drinking in the beach park parking lot. But real beer was not acceptable. We would never consider drinking on duty. But beer bottles would be great props, so we searched the garbage cans for old beer bottles. We stood outside Allen's old Chevy Blazer, which he used for fishing. The beer bottles stood on the hood of the car, exactly where a couple of guys enjoying the night and some brews would put them. We were convinced that we now looked like two guys drinking at the park.

You know, when you stand outside a vehicle with old almost-empty beer bottles for long hours into the night, watching a target location and talking about a thousand things with your partner, you tend to forget that the beer bottle you palmed with your hand once belonged to someone else and recently came out of a garbage can. I must have been thirsty. In a movement that seemed completely normal, I brought the beer bottle to my lips and took a sip of its contents. And started to swallow. The act of violently spitting out whatever liquid I just took into my mouth and throat was also understandable and normal. My partner's loud sustained laughter over the next few minutes was also predictable and understandable and normal. My mind was racing as to what might have been in that bottle, hoping beyond hope that it was nothing but old, stale beer. But I was losing the battle with my stomach, even though just a tad bit of liquid made it down my throat. I proceeded to the next level of normal behavior and got very queasy. Trying to clean the interior of my mouth, I continued to spit over the next hour or so, and was miserable for the remainder of the night.

The stakeout continued for a few more nights without any activity, and we were beginning to think we had chosen the wrong potential victim. Then suddenly, at about 1 a.m., we heard one of the officers call over the radio that a man had just entered the property.

We all got very excited. But before any burglary occurred, the man apparently suspected a trap. Perhaps he saw someone. Perhaps he just had a sense that he was walking into an ambush. He turned and ran out of the property and into the lane. The officers gave chase. The man, instead of running on the roadway, ran through people's yards and jumped their walls and fences. The officers pursued, but this suspect knew the area. And he apparently knew it very well. Because of this the edge went to him, and he quickly disappeared. We knew he had probably suspected that the police were trying to catch him because of his burglaries and threats, but now we had made that very clear to him. And we had failed to catch him. We were not supposed to fail. The police cannot fail. The community expects us to win. Every time.

We didn't know what he would do next. Would he lie low? Would he step up his activity to flaunt his escape and taunt the police? We could only wait and see.

Losing the suspect was a blow. Prior to that stakeout, we had no idea who our panty burglar was. He came within a few feet of police officers and successfully slipped through our grasp. We still had no idea who he was. We had no idea what he looked like. He was no more than a shadow in the dark. An outline in the night. A deviant, about to commit his crime, but sensing a trap, flew from the outstretched arms of his potential captors. We felt this failure deeply.

We felt it even more when we were assigned a new burglary case.

We needed to try something new. One of the past victims who kept in touch with us offered to ask her uncle if we could rent his house on Kāhala Beach for a different type of stakeout to catch the panty burglar. But we didn't want simply to wait for the burglar to hit again; we wanted to draw him in. We wanted to give him a target to attack. So we negotiated a fair rent for the house for a two-week period. Our bosses agreed to pay for both the rent and the overtime.

The plan was complex. We would rent the house and set the trap. But first we needed the bait. Literally. The term "bait" is not used here in a sexist manner. It is used to describe how we intended to lure the suspect into the open so we could close the trap and make our arrest. We needed a woman to lure him in. Obviously, we could not ask a civilian to take this risk, so we searched the ranks of the department for a woman who fit the description of the burglar's victims. We were looking for a young, pretty policewoman. We found one. Then one of the detectives looked at her picture and commented, "What if he doesn't want to go after a blonde this time?" So we looked again and found a brunette as well.

Our plan consisted of putting three or four officers in the house, some of whom would be detectives. The Honolulu District Crime Reduction Unit—a plainclothes unit—provided chase cars, and Fourth Watch foot-patrol officers were ready to chase on foot. We had the women officers wear swimsuits as often as possible. Their assignment was to walk, jog, and bike along Kāhala Avenue, and swim and sun themselves on Kāhala Beach. We wanted them to be seen by as many people as possible and hoped one of those people would be the panty burglar, who would follow them home.

Inside the house we would remain unseen, waiting for the burglar to break in to steal a pair of panties or two. We took enough food and other supplies to keep us from having to leave the house and possibly expose our trap. We also had cameras and tape recorders ready. We really wanted to catch this guy.

The officers inside the house included me, Allen, and a partner in the East Honolulu Burg/Theft Zone, Detective Cliff. Cliff was a hard-working detective who loved the water and loved to dive. He loved the water so much that his nickname was "Turtle." Turtle was told up front that it would be his task to chase the suspect if the suspect went into the ocean.

Trying to remain unseen inside a house is much more difficult than it would seem. You've got to stay away from doors and windows, which means you slink and move furtively. It also means that you sit still for long periods. Your ears become your eyes to the world outside. The officers who were assigned to foot or chase car positions occasionally conversed over the radio about suspicious people that they saw. We used a special radio channel so as not to interfere with day-to-day operations. And as we listened to these conversations, we occasionally provided some opinion or other input. It made us feel like we were actually involved in the stakeout.

We were wrong on one issue. The amount of food we brought wasn't enough. Because we were confined to the house, we depended on the shopping skills of the two policewomen who were our bait. Each of us in the house had our own preferences in food and drink, and we asked the women to buy a variety of items. Our grocery list often looked like conflicting restaurant menus. At first, we tried to keep our expense accounts straight by having the policewomen pay for our different items separately. That plan got thrown out real quick, after several awkward moments at the supermarket. So we pooled our money and learned to live with the culinary tastes of others.

The old house we rented had two bathrooms. One was designated for the women and the other for the men. We had a washer and a dryer, and each person was expected to take care of his or her own laundry. That was difficult, since we had only the one set of clothes we were wearing when we started the self-imposed confinement. So the men usually got their laundry done when the women were out of the house. to avoid embarrassing moments.

One phenomenon occurred that we didn't catch on to at first. None of the men wanted to sleep. During the day, as I mentioned, the foot and chase car officers monitored and discussed beachside and street activity. Our suspect had in the past made contact with victims during the day. But he attacked during the night. So during the day we listened to the outside conversations to see if we could pick out some important item that perhaps the chase officers might miss, and during the night we stayed awake, in case the suspect managed to slip into the house. We decided we would allow the suspect to actually burglarize the house before we would attempt to arrest him. This meant that the people in the house would not have the immediate assistance of "fresh" officers at the outside posts. Those outside assignments were rotated to keep those officers strong and alert. None of us inside the house feared the burglar. But we feared our stiff legs and backs, and worried that he would outrun us simply because our muscles were sore and unused.

After the first week, when we finally acknowledged that we were not supermen, we forced ourselves to sleep, one at a time, with the promise from the others that if there was any activity inside or outside the house, the sleeping detective would be awakened immediately. We started to feel a little refreshed, but with that came a growing frustration that we were halfway through our planned stakeout and still no closer to getting the suspect to take the bait and enter our snare.

Then one of the women reported a strange occurrence. She walked nonchalantly from the beach through the backyard and into the house. We were in our secluded positions, unseen from the windows. She walked to the kitchen sink, filled a glass with water, and gave us the news just as she started to drink.

"There's a naked man in the bushes alongside of the house."

She put the water glass down and casually walked back outside and lay down on the sand. The detectives inside the house began to coordinate outside activities to get more information and to try and identify the man.

"Hotel-One to Foxtrot-Alpha, go down one block on Kāhala Avenue, then go down the public access to the beach. Come back on the beach, walk past the house, and see if you can find this guy."

"Ten-four."

Minutes passed. Too many minutes. "What's taking this footman so long?" we asked ourselves. We were excited and antsy over the fact that we finally had some activity.

"Foxtrot-Alpha, the guy is in the *naupaka* bushes. He's naked. He's masturbating. You want me to go back and grab him?" asked the eager young officer.

"No!" came a chorus of voices—only one of which made it across the radio frequency. "No, keep walking and go back to the street at the next beach access."

We set up other officers along Kāhala Avenue and signaled the women to come inside. After a quick debriefing, we instructed the women to take a radio in a towel, go back to the beach, and sit in the lawn chairs. They were to notify us when the man left.

It wasn't long before one of the women officers called to report that the man had put on a pair of shorts and had come out of the bushes. He walked down the beach to the public access and disappeared. A minute later we got another transmission that a chase car had the suspect in sight. The man walked to a car, got in, and drove off. Officers in the chase car got his license number and begin tailing the vehicle. When the car reached the H-1 freeway, we instructed the chase car to let him go. From the vehicle's license number, we now had a name, and we could work on that.

Over the next few days, this man returned to the beach each morning. He went into some brush and removed his shorts. Sometimes he walked naked to the water and then went swimming. Other times, he simply remained in the *naupaka* bushes.

The woman who arranged the use of the beach house we used lived in a cottage behind it. She knew we had a possible suspect, but knew nothing else. She came to us in the early evening shortly after we identified the man in the *naupaka* bushes and told us something interesting.

"I have a gift," she stated, almost embarrassed to say it. "Sometimes, I can sense when things are about to happen."

We let her talk, even though none of us believed in psychics.

"The man you are watching is coming to Kāhala right now, and he's coming on Diamond Head Road from Waikīkī. He's going to go to the beach."

We really appreciated this young woman's efforts to help us get the beach house, and none of us wanted to offend her, so we played along.

"Hotel-Three to Chase-Two. Please drive down to Diamond Head Road and Kāhala Avenue. Be on the lookout for the suspect's vehicle. He may be driving to Kāhala from Waikīkī."

We sat with the woman, talking, and after ten minutes Chase-Two called.

"Chase-Two to Hotel-Three, I have the suspect in his vehicle on Kāhala Avenue. He came from the Waikīkī area on Diamond Head Road."

"Okay, follow him and let us know what happens."

Stunned, we turned our conversation to this young woman's ability. How did she know? She couldn't say, but for most of her life she had a special gift. Occasionally she could tell what was about to happen. It was a *feeling* she had.

"Chase-Two to Hotel-Three, suspect parked on Kāhala near the beach access. He's walking toward the beach now."

We arranged a surveillance.

Now that we had a possible suspect, we begged our supervisors to try to find enough money to rent the house for another week. We were running out of time. The first two weeks were ending, but our suspect had done nothing yet. In addition, no other cases had occurred during our stakeout. If we had the right man, we needed more time to watch and hope he would walk into our trap.

We were partially successful. We got one more week. Period. Then we had to leave if nothing happened. No more money. No more authority to extend the surveillance.

The week passed slowly. We had the women officers do everything short of flirting with the suspect. They walked, they swam, they jogged. Nothing. No response from him. We began to think that perhaps he was playing some sort of game with us, pushing us to see just what we would do. We would do nothing. We were not about to burn our stakeout. The naked man on the beach was eventually served with a penal summons for his lewd behavior, but it turned out he wasn't our panty burglar after all. (He turned out, however, to be someone well known enough in the community at the time to get his arrest reported in the media.)

After the third week, we went home, frustrated and disappointed. We felt like failures. It had been nearly ten months since the first pair of panties was stolen from a clothesline, and we were no closer to identifying the suspect then we were that first day. No one slept well our first night back from the stakeout. At work the next day, we tried to get back into the groove of handling our day-to-day caseload.

Before long we got right back into the Kāhala Panty Burglar investigation. A new victim turned up. She was a tall, beautiful woman who worked at a jewelry shop at the Kāhala Hilton. There was one difference between her and the other victims. She lived in a small cottage at the beginning of Kāhala Avenue, near Diamond Head Road. Far from the other crime scenes.

And her case would change everything in this investigation. It was about to take on a new dimension.

Violence.

5

The Kāhala Panty Burglar—Part Two

We met with Linda at the small, expensive jewelry shop at the Kāhala Hilton. She was dressed impeccably. Perfect for the clientele at the hotel. She had an air about her that caused people to take a second look. Unfortunately, the Kāhala Panty Burglar also liked what he saw.

Linda told us that she came home one day and found that someone had broken into her house. She didn't realize what was stolen until she got a telephone call from a man who told her he took her panties. She checked and found some of her panties missing. In addition, she had heard from friends that there was a guy stealing women's panties in Kāhala, so she called the police. The beat officer called us. We processed the scene, but found nothing we could use as evidence.

We told her, "Call us if you get any more calls or if you have any more problems." We advised her how to be careful and how to secure her home.

When several weeks went by and we hadn't heard from her, we felt and hoped that things were slowing down. Then one morning, our lieutenant informed us of the bad news.

"Remember that woman, a couple of weeks back? The one who worked at the Kāhala Hilton?"

"Yeah."

"She's in critical condition at the hospital. Someone entered her house and beat her over the head with a concrete tile block."

Did the panty burglar do this to her? Was it someone else? The lieutenant could see we were stunned.

"General Detail is handling."

"Was she raped?" came our next logical question.

"Don't know. They're trying to save her life, right now. Whoever did this bashed her face in and hurt her pretty bad."

The lieutenant was thinking what we were thinking—that the panty burglar's crimes had escalated to violence.

He told us, "Go talk to the General Detail and see what they have; maybe we can help."

When we spoke to the detectives of the General Detail, the detail that handles assaults, we learned that they too, had little evidence. Linda was found in the morning after she failed to come to work and didn't answer her telephone. Someone had entered her house, perhaps through a poorly secured front door. Perhaps he took a concrete tile block into the house, while Linda was sleeping. The block was the type used to build walls, sixteen inches long by eight inches wide and deep. Someone slammed it into her face many times. The bones in her face were crushed, and doctors feared she would lose her sight. But their first concern was whether she would survive. She was in a coma from the time she was found.

We joined in the investigation, but were of no real use to the General Detail guys. We had no firm information on any possible suspect. Could the Kāhala Panty Burglar have been responsible for Linda's assault? We didn't know and couldn't connect the cases. Weeks went by. There were no additional panty burglar cases. This only added to our suspicion. Was our suspect hiding out because he had nearly killed Linda? When she finally came out of the coma, she had no memory of the incident.

If the panty burglar was indeed responsible for Linda's assault, he was exhibiting behavior associated with escalating violent sexual offenses. Years later when I learned more about sexual predators and murderers, I learned that the fantasies of such people become more elaborate and more violent. I learned that this type of offender would probably not stop attacking women, and that his behavior would get worse. More important, I learned that sexuality to this kind of man was not what society believed to be normal.

In hindsight, it was apparent that the panty burglar's desire was to terrorize his victims. All along, his underlying motive was to have control over and to dominate his victims through fear. He terrorized by taking a very personal article of clothing. He terrorized by entering the women's homes while they slept. He terrorized by calling them and threatening them.

What we knew at the time was that we were very angry. What we knew was that this man was terrorizing the people who depended on the police to keep them safe. And so far we had failed. It was no longer just a job. It had long ago become a mission. And now it seemed to us to be a life or death struggle. Our obsession with the series of offenses kept us alert and continually thinking of new ways to catch this man.

Linda's case at the Waikīkī end of Kāhala Avenue wasn't the only one. We had another just off Diamond Head Road. And we began to conduct more stakeouts at this new house. Again, no luck. Perhaps this man was getting very good at smelling a trap, because the pace of offenses picked up again. Another victim, another burglary. This time, he went back to Kāhala Avenue nearer the Kāhala Hilton. But this latest victim was different. She wasn't afraid. She was angry. Angry that her privacy was invaded. And she was ready to fight back.

Maureen lived alone in a small two-bedroom, one-bath house. She worked in the downtown Honolulu area and had a boyfriend. One day she returned home to find that her home had been entered; some panties were missing. She reported the case, and we began the investigation, adding her to the long list of other victims. When we asked her if we could put a stakeout at her house, she said sure, she'd like to see the guy caught. But we didn't act quickly enough.

Before we could organize a stakeout, she called us back. Her voice was a little shaky, and she sounded upset. But she told us that it was because she was very angry, not afraid, and she really wanted to catch this guy now. She told us that the night before, she had gone to the movies with her boyfriend. They came back to her house and watched some television in the living room. After a while, they went to the bedroom and had sex. Afterward, they talked for a little while, and then her boyfriend left for his own apartment. She showered, then went to sleep.

Maureen told us that she woke up in the morning with the telephone ringing. She was groggy when she reached for the telephone and had a difficult time lifting the receiver. This caused her to wake up and pay a little more attention. She saw that a pair of her panties had been pulled down over her telephone. She pulled the panties away and lifted the receiver.

"Hello?"

"I watched you f— your boyfriend last night. The next guy you f— is going to be me. And it's going to be soon."

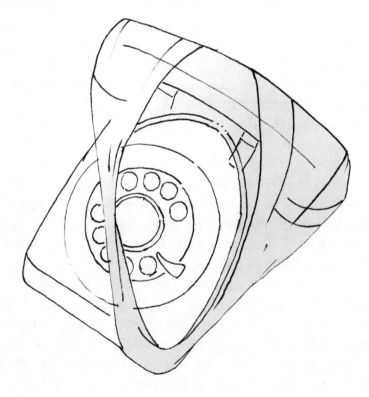

Maureen's panties pulled over her telephone

Maureen realized right away that this was probably the same man who had burglarized her house before. She knew that he apparently stood outside—and inside—her house watching her. She also knew that he was trying to terrorize her, and that he might try to make good on his threat someday. She called the police. "I'm not afraid," she told us again. She said she was mad as hell and wanted to see him arrested.

Our team of detectives and Kāhala officers got together and formed a stakeout plan. This time we were all volunteering, because the department had no more money for overtime stakeouts. Because of the dedication of the beat officers, we developed a team that would watch Maureen's house.

Since we had limited personnel, our stakeout was a simple one. We had one officer in a chase car and two in the tall hedge that surrounded her house. The hedge was leafy, but there was enough room just behind it for an officer to sit between the hedge and the neighbor's chain-link fence. We put one officer on either side of her house and the chase car in a lane across from her driveway. Enough of us had volunteered to allow two teams, and so we switched off each day. One team entered the hedge just before dark and worked until dawn, while the other team rested.

Sitting on a stakeout can be exciting. It can also be terribly boring. Ninety-nine percent of the time we're waiting and watching. When we're in the brush we can't leave, so we bring everything we'll need to provide comfort for eight to ten hours. Besides our police radio, gun, and handcuffs, we bring a knapsack of soda, water, and food— quiet food. We don't want to be crunching on chips while hiding in the brush. We also don't want to eat food that will require us to rush to a bathroom. Since it is not healthy, and probably not possible, to refrain from relieving ourselves for ten hours, the solution is to bring a container. Like our canine friends, we don't want to mess where we're going to sit. We also don't want to be walking through the brush to find another location, and we certainly don't want to sit in the mess of another officer who was there the night before. So we learn to relieve ourselves into a container while sitting cross-legged on the ground. Two goals: don't splash on the ground and definitely not on our clothes. We'll be sitting in those clothes for a number of hours. Cleanliness and consideration for other officers are important factors.

One evening just after it got dark, I was settling in and trying to get comfortable. I opened my knapsack and took out a sandwich. I remember clearly it was a deli turkey sandwich with mayonnaise and a slice of American cheese. I made it myself. I took one bite and heard a soft, low, rumbling growl coming from my left. I looked and saw a large dog lying on the dirt a few feet away. He was a mixed breed, probably part pit-bull, part mutt, and he looked at me with a face that said, *You're not going to eat that alone, are you?* I broke off a piece of the sandwich and tossed it to the dog. He swallowed it whole and moved closer. I took a bite and then his eyes said, *My turn.* We shared that sandwich and, a little later, we shared another. By the end of the night, he had his head in my lap and I was scratching behind his ears. We shared food, water, and company. At the end of the shift, I actually thought that if I had to chase after the panty burglar, the dog would chase him as well. So I deputized him and named him Deputy Dawg. As I left the brush the next morning, I told Dawg that I would see him in a couple of days. I was truly disappointed that I never saw him again. I guess his owner was worried when he didn't come home that night and locked him up when he finally did.

A few nights later, the second team was working the stakeout and I was out on the road. It was late and very quiet. I was driving near Hawai'i Kai getting ready to go home when I heard the radio conversation that sent my blood pressure skyrocketing.

"Chase-One to Hotel-One, there's a male walking toward the house."

The chase car had the assignment to notify the officers in the brush every time someone walked near the house. It helped the guys in the brush to stay alert. At that moment, no one really got excited. There had been many notifications that people were walking near the house during the last week.

What I didn't know from my position on the roadway was that Maureen was awake. She got up to go to the bathroom. The house was dark, however, except for the bathroom light.

"Chase-One . . . he just turned into the driveway! I lost him!"

I sped toward Kāhala, running red lights and overtaking slower-moving vehicles. The detective's voice was strained with excitement. At the same time, Hotel-One, the officer in the brush across the driveway, also saw the man. But he couldn't speak. The man was about thirty feet away, and the officer didn't want to risk being heard. The man, who was slender, had dark hair, and wore dark clothing, suddenly, disappeared around the front of the house, moving out of the view of Hotel-One. Again, the officers had to count on their own alertness, because no one could speak for fear of revealing themselves. The first two officers couldn't know that Hotel-Two actually watched the man come around the front of the house and walk toward the light of the bathroom, moving to within fifteen feet of his position.

While this was going on, I was hoping against hope that this wasn't just a passerby who needed to relieve himself in the shadows of the tall brush.

The man walked up to the bathroom window. The window ledge was low enough so that the man's eyes were just above the ledge and he could see into the house. Maureen was in the bathroom relieving herself. The male began to rub his groin. In a moment he undid his belt and loosened his pants. He began to masturbate. His other hand was reaching to the window screen.

The first two officers were almost overwhelmed with stress, not knowing what was going on out of their view, but knew that it was critically important to maintain their positions.

Suddenly, a blood-curdling scream filled the air. It was described later as sounding like someone had just fallen off a cliff. Hotel-One burst from the hedge opposite the driveway and sprinted around the house. Chase-One saw this and drove his car across the street.

Glass shattered. Hotel-One said later that when the glass shattered he pulled his gun from his holster, not knowing what to expect. When he turned the corner, he saw Hotel-Two struggling to finish handcuffing the man, who was lying on the ground.

We learned later that Hotel-Two, a young officer, couldn't contain himself any longer as he watched the man masturbate and try to reach into the house. He charged from the hedge toward the man. The male turned and looked as if he was about to put up a fight, in spite of the fact that his pants and underwear were pulled down around his hips. The officer grabbed him, and in a brief struggle they slammed into the glass of the window, breaking it.

In the surprise of the officer's rush toward him, the suspect lost control of his bodily functions and defecated on himself and in his pants. He was arrested for trespass, and we called for a blue-and-white car to transport him to the Receiving Desk. As we talked among ourselves after the male was driven off to the station, we finally learned the entire sequence of events. But we had to ask.

"Why did the guy scream?"

"He didn't scream," came an embarrassed answer. "I guess it was me as I ran at him out of the bushes. I'm sorry."

"Nothing to be sorry at. You caught him."

We were excited. We thought we had the panty burglar. It was hard to not feel that we had finally ended what we thought was a year-long curse. Maureen was excited. She couldn't go back to sleep, so she made some coffee and kept our cups filled as we processed her house with the evidence specialists.

By the end of the next day, we knew for sure. The suspect wouldn't talk to us. He invoked the Fifth Amendment and demanded an attorney. But it didn't matter. We had positive fingerprint comparisons, putting him inside the homes of several victims. He was going to be convicted, confession or not.

The latent fingerprints recovered from Linda's house, however, did not match the inked fingerprints taken from the arrested man, and we couldn't prove that he was the person who entered her home and assaulted her with the concrete-tile block.

The investigation took over a year. There were multiple victims, seemingly unending stress, but persistence and dedication by a lot of beat officers and detectives finally paid off.

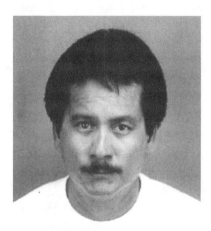

The mug photograph of Harrison Mew

Harrison Mew, a Pālolo resident at the time, was arrested, charged, and convicted for those panty burglaries in Kāhala after the investigation proved that his fingerprints matched those found at some of the crime scenes. Mew was sentenced to ten years in prison for those crimes. He served his full term and was released back into the community.

6
The Lust Murder of Robin Bayliss

Murder is murder, each one just another case, investigated the same way by detectives as every other one, right? Truth is, it's never that simple. Each case has its own dynamics that make it different from any other. While all murder investigations do have similar basic crime-scene responsibilities, the motive in certain types of cases may help detectives direct follow-up work.

Sexual homicide is a type of murder in which an understanding of motive is important to solving the case. Sexual homicides vary widely, from rape that turns into unintentional murder to serial killings. As defined by various scholars: Sexual homicide is an act of control, dominance, and performance that is representative of an underlying fantasy embedded with violence, sexuality and death. Sexuality in the context of this definition is not that which society considers normal. Sexuality, in this case, comes in the form of violence, torture, and the creation of great fear in the victim. Dominance over the victim is a critically important aspect of the killer's deviant sexuality. The greater the torment the killer can inflict on the victim, the greater his sexual high in some cases. One example of the sexual homicide is the lust murder.

In the realm of homicide classifications, the lust murder falls into the seemingly simple *single murder* category as a sexual killing. A killer murders one victim in the course of one event at one location, unlike a serial killer, who murders again and again.

The lust murder is a particularly brutal crime. It often involves the stalking of a woman from a distance. She has no idea that someone is stalking her. Unlike the Kāhala Panty Burglar (see chapters 4 and 5), who terrorized his victims over the telephone, the lust murderer fantasizes from afar, building his deviant dreams until he bursts into reality and kills. Some people say, "This is Hawai'i. This doesn't happen here." Unfortunately, it does. While some detectives disagree, it seems apparent that we have had at least one lust murder in Honolulu.

Robin Bayliss was a young woman who worked as a secretary for her boyfriend's door-to-door sales company, Wholesale Warehouse Industries, on Leoleo Street in Waipahu. She came to Hawai'i from Canada in February of 1988, met her boyfriend, and began working at his business. On August 23, 1988, after her boyfriend and all the other salespeople picked up their goods and left for their routes, Bayliss was viciously attacked in the warehouse of the business and left for dead. That afternoon, at 4:45, she was found stabbed and bleeding by a returning salesman, who called for an ambulance and the police. Bayliss, who never regained consciousness, died at The Queen's Medical Center two days later.

To the lust murderer, the infliction of the injuries is, in a perverse way, sexual. The attack, the brutal assault, and the infliction of multiple injuries come together in the form of control over the life or death of the victim. The killer is attracted to his victim from afar. He strikes without warning and he flees as quickly as he kills. He is difficult to identify. He is difficult to catch. And he leaves few clues for the police to work with.

But nothing about Bayliss's murder indicated a sexual assault—no rape, that is. Her injuries, however, had all the makings of a lust assault. Her assailant stabbed her repeatedly in her face, her breasts, and her vagina. While there was no evidence of a sexual assault in the typical sense—no rape, no seminal fluid—the attack on Bayliss was indeed sexual.

She was attacked with a Phillips screwdriver–like weapon, information that the investigators tried—unsuccessfully—to keep from the media. A few days after the attack, the police department unveiled its program to change the weapon used by officers from the .38-caliber revolver to the .9-mm semi-automatic handgun. At the news conference at which Chief Douglas Gibb announced the changeover, a reporter asked about the status of the "stabbing" investigation. Chief Gibb, who apparently was confused about which case the reporter was referring to, asked if the reporter was referring to the woman stabbed with the Phillips screwdriver. This was the first that the reporters had heard about the weapon used in the Bayliss murder, and investigators still wanted to keep that information confidential. Only the deceased victim, the investigators, and the killer knew the type of weapon used. Once Gibb saw the reaction of the reporters, he realized that he had inadvertently released information that should never have been given to the media. Unfortunately, after that, every media account of the Bayliss murder included a description of the murder weapon.

The media also learned, from an employee in the medical examiner's office, that Bayliss died of penetrating stab wounds to the head and brain and that she had cross-shaped abrasions to her face, neck, and chest. This kind of unthinking release of information without discussing it with investigators can have disastrous effects on an investigation.

After the diagrams and photos of the crime scene are complete, evidence is collected and preserved with a chain of custody. "Chain of custody" is a concept that protects the integrity of evidence. It is an accounting of all the people who have come into contact with the evidence, whether they examined, tested, or simply stored the evidence. The chain begins when the evidence is discovered and continues through presentation at court.

An interesting aspect of the investigation came during the crime scene processing. Bayliss was found lying on the concrete floor of the warehouse where she worked. The floor was smooth, finished concrete, not the rough surface found on driveways and roadways.

Because it was smooth, we thought it was possible to find finger-prints that might have been left by her killer. So our evidence specialist got down on his knees and, beginning at the entrance to the warehouse, worked his way across the room, slowly and deliberately looking for latent fingerprints. Some fingerprints were indeed discovered, but since police have no suspect to compare them with, they remain filed, waiting for the day when they can be compared.

Because the warehouse's concrete floor was dark gray, the evidence specialist dusting for prints used a fluorescent powder and an ultraviolet light to locate the latent prints. In addition to the prints, he discovered something unusual. Whenever he directed the ultraviolet light near the spot where Bayliss's body had lain, he discovered, on the concrete, a yellowish-greenish glow that resembled a skull. The concrete was dry, and whenever he removed the ultraviolet light the glow disappeared. It was not visible in normal incandescent lighting. The evidence specialists puzzled over this, thinking that perhaps there was something in the concrete itself that created the glow, but that didn't seem reasonable. We applied the light again and took photos of the eerie, glowing spot. It wasn't until later, after Bayliss's autopsy, that we discovered the cause of the glowing skull-like stain. The post-mortem examination and lab results showed that Bayliss had a prescription medication in her blood, medication she was taking for a minor ailment. One of the evidence specialists suggested that perhaps the medication interacted with her blood and caused it to fluoresce. The only problem was that there was no dried blood where the glowing spot was located. Someone suggested it was urine. We checked with the paramedics and learned that there was some urine on the floor where Bayliss lay. It's common in assaults such as Bayliss endured for the victim to lose continence. Our next question to the lab was "Would the medication Bayliss was taking cause her urine to fluoresce in the presence of ultraviolet light?" The answer was yes.

This discovery is an example of another important type of evidence from crime scenes: serology, generally known as the study of blood, blood serum, and other body fluids. Blood, as evidence, can tell us a lot. Reconstruction of the bloodstain pattern in Roland Kotani's murder (see Chapter One) helped us reconstruct the events surrounding his death. ABO typing gives us one of the four blood-types, A, B, AB, and O. Blood type can also be determined using body fluids such as perspiration, saliva, semen, and vaginal secretions if the person is a secretor. Secretors are persons who have ABO blood grouping material in those body fluids.

ABO typing is not as useful as DNA typing. Blood types A and O are the most common, together found in 82 percent of the population. DNA typing provides a much more conclusive result, even though it is not considered absolute, as fingerprints are. The DNA, or deoxyribonucleic acid, molecule is commonly described as a double helix, looking like a ladder that has been twisted. Scientists can examine pieces of DNA, look for similarities, and make precise comparative statements, such as "one person in several billion would share this DNA."

A very important class of evidence in Bayliss's case was trace evidence. Based on the scientific principle of material transfer developed by French scientist Edmund Locard, "trace evidence" is a generic term for small, often microscopic evidence. Locard's Transfer Principle states that when two objects come into contact with each other, a partial transfer of material occurs, and each object leaves evidence of its presence on the other. Some examples of trace evidence are hair, fibers, and arson char.

Since investigators didn't know exactly what happened during Bayliss's assault, finding trace evidence was important. Trace evidence is primarily a comparison-based field. Items found at a crime scene can be compared with items on a suspect or from a suspect's house or car. The criminalist doing the comparison can then state that the evidence resembles the sample in specific characteristics.

⊕

One conclusion was evident to some of the investigators: Bayliss's murder was sexual.

Sexual killers are usually men. The serial killer Ted Bundy once remarked to detectives that he experienced an extremely high level of sexual excitement and arousal when he felt his victims' saliva or vomit flow over his hands as he strangled them. In an interview with an investigator he bragged, "What greater power can one have than power over life and death?" Remember that the definition of sexual homicide is based on control, dominance, and violence, including death.

At a homicide seminar held at the New York State Police Academy I heard a talk by Dr. Park Deitz, an internationally known psychiatrist who has studied sexual murderers and serial killers. Dietz believes that sexual and serial killers are not psychotic. They all have, he said, some mental or personality disorder in the area of sexuality, but they're not insane. Each knows right from wrong. And each knows that what he's doing is wrong. This is why serial killers brought to trial are often convicted rather than being found legally insane.

One problem with lust murders and other sexual homicides that may not exhibit any sexual indication is that the police may not identify them as sexual homicides. An example of this, presented at an FBI homicide seminar in Quantico Virginia, was a prostitute found in an alley with her throat cut. There was no evidence of any sexual assault. Investigators concluded that she was murdered by a john who refused to pay. In reality, she was the victim of a lust murderer. Only when other prostitutes were found murdered in a similar fashion did investigators suspect a sexual serial killing.

So how does a person become this extraordinarily cruel monster? Does he wake up one morning and decide that he will embark on a journey to cause anguish and murder? In their book *Sexual Homicide: Patterns and Motives,* Robert Ressler, Ann Burgess, and John Douglas present a motivational model describing the development of a person who may have tendencies toward becoming a sexual murderer. They acknowledge that this is only a model: some killers—Ted Bundy, for example—may not fit the model.

In this model, a child grows up in an ineffective social environment in which the child's bad behavior is ignored to the point of non-intervention by parents or guardians. Formative events may include physical and sexual abuse. With no role models and subject to frequent abuse, the child develops a diminished emotional response; that is, the child feels less and less emotion toward events that would evoke fear, shame, or guilt, for example, in people with normal emotions.

These childhood events develop into a set of patterned responses such as social isolation, lying, compulsive masturbation, and entitlement—not the sense of entitlement in which a person may feel that society owes him a living, but an entitlement that expresses the belief that "I can do whatever I want without consequence." Other patterned responses involve abuse, fire starting, animal torture, assaults, and other crimes that have power, dominance, and violence as themes. These patterned responses further develop into sexually oriented violent behaviors such as rape. And it is important to remember here that rape is also an offense in which the perpetrator has a diminished emotional response, and where dominance over the victim is a key factor.

The deviant person, in a model devised by the FBI, develops a fantasy. Now we all fantasize and daydream. There is nothing wrong with that. J. L. Singer, in the book *Daydreams*, defines "daydreams" as any cognitive activity representing a shift of attention away from a task. The *Journal of Interpersonal Violence* defines "fantasy" as a conscious thought with great preoccupation anchored with emotion and having origins in daydreams. But the sexual murderer uses this process of fantasy to create a blueprint—the set of plans that tell him who his victim should be, how to select and abduct the victim, how to commit the murder, whether he will inflict torture or not, and on and on.

The development of a serial killer occurs over time. The killer's fantasies become more and more elaborate. These deviants may start their journey toward murder with fetishes, obsessing over women's shoes or panties or something else. But as their fantasies grow, their crimes expand. Soon the fantasy can no longer satisfy their deviant sexual needs, and the murders begin. The FBI identified a cooling-off period between killings. The pattern is described as being like a wave. The fantasy grows and peaks and a murder occurs, satisfying the killer's deviant sexual urges. It then wanes. Slowly the fantasy builds again, growing to new proportions and a greater degree of elaboration. It peaks again and another murder occurs. And the cycle continues.

In normal life, people review their work or other activity in an effort to become better at what they do. The sexual serial killer does the same thing. He uses a review the FBI calls a "feedback filter" to justify his acts, further develop his elaborate fantasy, increase his pleasure, and find ways to continue his terror without getting caught.

At a training seminar I attended at the FBI Academy, one instructor stated that—based on the definition given above—all serial killings are sexual homicides. The reverse, however, isn't true. Not all sexual homicides are, or become, serial killings.

The FBI has also broken sexual murders and murderers into two classifications: organized and disorganized. The organized killer plans his offense, demands a submissive victim, uses restraints, controls his acts and crime scenes, and may transport the body of his victim. He often also hides the body, performs aggressive acts prior to the murder, and takes the weapon or other evidence away from the crime scene.

In contrast, the disorganized killer often shows little planning, committing his crimes spontaneously. His crime scene is random and sloppy. He may even know his victim. He often leaves the body, as well as other evidence and weapons, within view. While he rarely uses restraints, he may leave evidence of sexual acts committed after the victim is dead.

Robin Bayliss was murdered by an organized killer. The murder weapon was not found with the body, and the assault took place in relatively safe surroundings—safe in the sense that the killer had time to commit his act without being seen by the public.

One item of evidence that is frequently seen in sexual murders is bitemarks. Bitemarks can be recovered from many things that people bite: apples, cheese, Styrofoam cups, and even other human beings. Bitemarks made on human skin continue to develop even after death, and documentation requires extensive photography over a period of days as the telltale bruising develops.

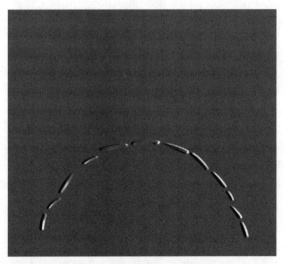

An example of bitemark impressions in wax

Even when the person who was bitten survives and the bitemarks heal, photographs of the scarring underneath the top layers of skin can be made using ultraviolet light. Bitemarks found on a dead body are photographed in both color and black-and-white, on a 1:1 basis. Bitemarks that leave depressions in the skin can be cast, using dental stone, the same material dentists use to cast teeth.

When an arrested suspect is suspected of having bitten his victim, a forensic odontologist is called into the investigation. The odontologist takes impressions of the suspect's teeth and compares them to the photographs of the bitemarks. Because bitemarks are unique, in some cases such evidence is considered as reliable as fingerprints.

Sexual murders have four basic phases. The first is *antecedent behavior*. During this phase the killer selects his victim. The organized killer goes looking for his victim, while the disorganized killer may depend on some environmental cue to choose his. For example, the organized killer goes to a bar on Monday night. A football game is on TV. He sits at the bar and orders a beer. While the other people may be cheering on their favorite team, the organized killer is searching the room for a possible victim. Once he makes his selection, there is little she can do to escape his plans. Some of these organized killers have selection criteria when choosing a victim. Ted Bundy selected victims who had long dark hair parted in the middle. The disorganized killer, on the other hand, goes to the same bar, orders a beer, and sits back and enjoys the ball game. Thoroughly satisfied, he pays his bill and leaves. As he drives from the bar, he sees a woman hitchhiking, and his environmental cue goes off. He stops, she gets in, and his sexually murderous fantasy begins.

During the second phase, the killer commits the murder. He acts out his fantasy. One problem he faces, however, is that during the early stage of a serial killer's career, the actual act of murder may be extremely different from what he fantasizes it will be. Killing someone with one's hands is much more difficult than Hollywood makes it seem, and the sexual killer may experience this difficulty. The victim may scream and fight back—gouge, scratch, bite, kick—or do anything else to escape the killer. If the murderer is successful, even though the killing was very difficult to accomplish, he will use his feedback filter to look for ways to "improve" future murders so they occur with fewer complications. Investigators may see the use of restraints in future killings.

During the third phase of a sexual homicide the killer disposes of the body. Again, the fantasy plays a role here. The organized killer may transport and hide the body. The disorganized killer may leave the body at the scene of the murder.

The fourth phase includes postcrime behavior. In many instances, this involves the discovery of the body. The discovery of the killer's gruesome act extends his ability to control and dominate. With the finding of the body, the fear the killer created in his victim is transferred from the victim to the community. His power and domination now extend into the cities and suburbs where parents fear for their daughters' safety and the police seem stymied by the task of catching the man committing these horrendous murders. The killer's need for public acknowledgment of the crime may prompt him to plan for the discovery of the body. If the body is not immediately found, he may give clues to the police, and in rare instances, he may lead the police to his victim's body. This happened in the mid-1980s in Honolulu when a suspected serial killer came to the police to say a psychic told him where the body lay.

Unlike the Hollywood version of a serial killer—a physically aberrant deviant lurking in the shadows—many are handsome men, charming, charismatic, and easy to trust. Generally, they are intelligent. If they don't excel in intelligence, their street smarts make up for that deficiency. Many are attracted to law enforcement and are fascinated with police procedures. They understand forensic science and crime-scene investigations. Historically, their victims are vulnerable people such as children, prostitutes, and the elderly. They normally stick to one victim pattern and usually kill within their own race. It has been said that serial killing is a white man's crime because there have been so few black, Hispanic, or Asian serial killers. The serial killers' homicidal incidents accelerate until they are constantly looking for victims.

Many scholars, psychologists, and psychiatrists, along with the FBI and many police investigators, believe that a serial killer never stops killing until he gets caught, dies, or suffers some debilitating illness that prevents him from killing again. Rehabilitation of a serial killer is viewed as unlikely, if not impossible.

Serial killing and sexual homicide may be the most difficult types of murder to solve. They involve the killing of a stranger, by a stranger. Often there is little evidence left at the murder scene. The killers are monsters who may leave a trail of multiple victims. These killings leave a community in a vise-grip of fear. And they leave police investigators numb, lost in a dark abyss with little hope of success.

Robin Bayliss was a shy, pretty young woman described by friends as a person who preferred to stay at home after work. Three months after her murder, friends and family put together a $50,000 reward for information leading to the arrest and conviction of her killer. It was, at the time, the largest reward offered in Hawai'i.

Her murder remains unsolved.

7
Honolulu's Serial Killings

People in Honolulu pride themselves on living in a community that manages to have a small-town feel with some modern-day sophistication. We know we don't want to live in a big city indistinguishable from the next. We love our Costco, and even hit the fast-food places when we're short on time and money. We don't mourn for the days when television programs showed up a week after they appeared on the mainland. But we still depend on our neighborhood stores for our everyday needs and really rave about the okazu down the street or the reliable mom-and-pop restaurant. For the most part, we realize that the best part of that sense of community comes from people who generally feel connected to one another. And one area where we happily lag behind—most of the time—is crime. Sure, there have been murders here for as long as there have been people, but we still print the names of all murder victims in our daily newspapers. Most murders still get television coverage, something that sets people from big cities to shaking their heads.

And we pay attention to the crimes, searching for the connections. If we read a crime story, we try to figure out if that robbery happened near Auntie So-and-So's house in Kapahulu. If we watch news about a murder on TV, we listen for the victim's name. Hey, didn't she go to Roosevelt with that guy we used to work with at the supermarket? Or isn't that your mom's neighbors' grandson?

The specter of a faceless killer stalking victims and coldly killing them in some sort of pattern makes our blood run cold. Usually, that's something we see only in the movies or on television. That changed in 1985–86 when Honolulu became home to its first identified serial killer, a modern term we don't want to associate with our home. In our small town, many people had links to the victims.

During the serial killings, one newscaster reporting the death of the women realized that he had briefly dated one of the victims.

Within a year, five young women were dead, and Honolulu police found themselves searching for a serial killer straight out of the profile developed by the Federal Bureau of Investigations.

The women had some things in common: They had Caucasian features, they were generally young and not very tall, and most of the bodies were discovered in the same area, in or near water and near the Honolulu airport and Keʻehi Lagoon. At least three of them were bound with strapping tape. All of them had family or friends who cared about them. Some had experienced tough times in their lives, which led those around them to see them as less likely to be easy targets.

The killings were most horrifying for the families and friends of the young women, but the crimes reverberated beyond their circle, changing the way people lived and toughening them to a modern reality. Suddenly, it could happen here.

The first to die was Vicki Gail Purdy. She was twenty-five years old and lived in Mililani with her husband, Gary Purdy, who flew helicopters in the army. She was blonde and pretty and she worked at Wahiawa Video Rental. Friends and family said that she might look small at 5-feet-5 inches and 135 pounds, but she could be fierce.

Gary described his wife as tough, someone who took no grief from others and had "knocked the shit" out of him when they had marriage problems early in their relationship. The two had met back in Marietta, Georgia. At age sixteen—while still in high school— Vicki Gail Ezzell had married Purdy's cousin. Her stepbrother said that she and Gary got together after that relationship fell apart, after they graduated from high school, when Gary was preparing to enter the army.

Vicki Purdy was from a North Carolina family, but her parents divorced when she was quite young, her mother's subsequent marriage broke up, and Vicky lived in a foster home for a while, according to stepbrother James Foreman, who lived in Alabama at the time of her death. Foreman recalled his sister as someone who kept in touch with their mother, but grew apart from the family after marrying.

Foreman described Vicki as someone who had always wanted to move to Hawai'i, but found that life here wasn't quite what she expected. Foreman described her as outgoing, a former cheerleader who liked life on the go, but he thought that she fell in with the wrong kinds of friends in the islands.

Gary and Vicki had been married for five years when they moved to Hawai'i some sixteen months before her death. Gary told reporters that the two had bad times in their relationship, but things were looking up. At the time, he said, "She had a great love for life. She was the backbone of our family." Without her, he said, he would never have become an army officer.

He also described their marriage as "adventurous" and told investigators and reporters at the time that it wasn't unusual for Vicki to head to Waikīkī for an evening of nightclubbing with friends without him. He told police he kissed her good-bye early on a Wednesday evening and expected her home by about nine that night. When hours passed without her return, he began paging her again and again. The next day he frantically searched for her and found her car, newly dented, sitting in the parking garage of the old Shorebird Hotel. Friends said she had telephoned them at 10 P.M., but didn't meet them as planned. A cab driver told police he had driven her back to the Shorebird about midnight. She was wearing a yellow jumpsuit and a red belt.

Her body was found the next day. She had been raped, strangled, and dumped off an embankment at the edge of Ke'ehi Lagoon.

After her murder, her husband objected when people implied that his wife had worked at a sleazy place (because it rented X-rated videos). And he said he never knew that the Wahiawā store itself had been hit by violence less than a year before her murder. The December before Vicki Purdy was murdered, two women who worked there—a part-owner and an employee—were found stabbed to death in the store.

Vicki Purdy's death marked the beginning of what came to be known as the serial killings. But at the time, her death seemed far removed from the lives of most residents. Her husband was her only family here. He left after her death, vowing not to return unless her killer was brought to justice. It was difficult to find friends of hers willing to describe her, and the tumultuous and "adventurous" lifestyle her husband described further distanced most people from feeling that they shared very much with the young victim.

The next victim was Regina Sakamoto, the youngest of the women who died in those two years. She was seventeen years old, a Leilehua High School senior when she disappeared. School pictures of Regina show a pretty girl with dark blonde hair and a confident smile. She had the look of a girl who would succeed, who could easily gain friends. She was 4 feet 11 inches tall and weighed about 105 pounds.

Most of those who knew her well steered clear of the news media at the time of her death. Those who did talk about her after her tragic death painted her as a shy but friendly girl. A school adviser recalled her as kind and careful, close to her mother and at least one high school girlfriend.

Regina was born in Kansas when her mother—who was also named Regina—was married to a man named Ben Arnett. Regina Arnett met Maurice Sakamoto at a military base in California. Five-year-old Regina had been living with her grandmother. But after her mother married Sakamoto, he adopted her and helped raise her for the next ten years. The couple divorced when Regina was fifteen, and Sakamoto grew apart from his daughter, even though she continued to commute from her Waipahu home to Wahiawā, where he lived.

The divorce had left bad feelings. Sakamoto said he criticized his ex-wife for moving the two into a neighborhood he thought was seedy and unsafe. He had warned her mother that the fair and pretty teenager was a target in a community he thought was dangerous and filled with transients.

Regina was catching an early-morning bus to school from Waipahu when she disappeared. At about 7:15 that morning, she missed her bus and called her boyfriend from a phone booth to tell him she would be late for school. Her body was discovered the next day, January 15, also in Keʻehi Lagoon near the airport's reef runway. She was wearing a blue tank top and white Hawaiian Island Creations sweatshirt. She, too, had been raped and strangled. A homicide detective noticed the similarities between Sakamoto's killing and that of Purdy seven-and-a-half months earlier. But others in the police department doubted the link, and the public received no warning that the killings might be related.

Detectives in the cases could see evidence of the cause of death when they observed tiny red pinpoint marks on the face, the eyes, and the eyelids of the victims. These marks are called "petechial hemorrhaging" and are caused by pressure that occurs as a result of strangulation.

Other evidence that indicated the victims were strangled included a ligature furrow in the victims' necks, which occurs as a result of the pressure or tightness of the ligature around the neck. The furrow remains even after the rope or other binding is removed. Ligature furrows also occur when victims are bound on their arms and legs.

Just two weeks after Regina's body was found—on February 1, 1986—three youths fishing along a drainage canal in Māpunapuna's Moanalua Stream made a chilling discovery. They found a bundle wrapped in blue tarp floating near the shore. When they opened it, they saw the decomposing body of a young woman, which had apparently been rolled down the mud embankment. Her hands were tied behind her back, and she was wearing an azure dress. She had been strangled. This time the victim's name was Denise Hughes.

Four days later, on February 5, Honolulu police major Chester Hughes (no relation) announced that he had formed a task force to investigate the similarities among the three murders. Hughes then served as head of HPD's Criminal Investigative Division. He was a tall, kindly figure who kept in shape by jogging regularly with a group of fellow police officers.

Hughes was polite and friendly enough with reporters at a time when the official police position seemed to be to avoid speaking to the news media as much as possible. He also had perfected the art of speaking many words without actually imparting any useful information. And he could do so in such a way that a reporter could leave an interview with him at the police department with pages of notes, feeling that Hughes had answered many questions, then go back to the office to realize he had actually given out only tidbits of information in his answers. That ability was clearly prized by the police department at the time and was certainly a useful skill when investigators wanted to keep crucial details away from public scrutiny. Hughes was clearly uncomfortable with the role of media spokesperson, but he and others in the department realized that the community was getting nervous. Some things needed to be said. They just weren't quite sure how to strike the balance between adequately warning people that there was a killer on the loose and not inciting panic. And they needed to catch the killer.

Denise Hughes was the victim who forced the issue public. The twenty-one-year-old from Washington State had moved to Hawai'i just five months before her death. She worked as a secretary while her husband, Charles, served in the navy, stationed aboard a ship at Pearl Harbor. The two had met while she vacationed in Hawai'i several months before, and they married in Seattle before returning to the islands to live.

Denise smiles warmly from old photos. She had a round face and brown curly hair that fell to her shoulders. She stood 5 feet 8 inches tall and weighed 154 pounds.

She had been working as a secretary at a long-distance telephone company for about three months before her death and had quickly made friends who accompanied her on shopping trips and played racquetball with her. Her supervisor was amazed at her constant smile.

Denise had grown up in Everett, Washington. Her mother, Linda Jorg, was seventeen when Denise was born, and Denise was adopted at age six by the man her mother married that year. Her mother worried when her daughter moved to Hawai'i, believing she had married too young. Jorg also found the Pearl City street where the Hughes's lived too remote and noted that her daughter would time her departure from the house in the morning to meet the bus just as it arrived to prevent having to wait there alone.

Friends and family described her as outgoing, a hiker who liked to ski, worked all the way through high school, and was active in a young Christian church group. Her relatives and friends gathered seven thousand dollars to reward anyone who brought forth information that could lead to the conviction of the killer.

The fourth victim was Louise Medeiros, another woman whom friends and relatives described as having hard times in her life. She was twenty-five, unemployed, and lived in Waipahu. Louise left home as a teenager, never finished high school, and spent a lot of her young life wandering. On the night of Wednesday, March 26, 1986, Louise was on Kaua'i, where she had gone for the reading of her mother's will.

She had lived in Mākaha for a while and spent time living on the beach on the Leeward Coast. Her sister had cautioned her against waiting at bus stops at night, but Louise shrugged off the suggestion that she wait for a day flight, saying she wanted to get back to her three sons, who were staying with her boyfriend's family while she made the trip to visit with her large family on Kaua'i after the death of her mother.

She flew home to O'ahu, telling her family that she would catch a bus from the airport to the apartment she shared with her boyfriend in Waipahu. A single mother, Louise was 5 feet 4 inches tall, weighed less than 90 pounds, and was three months pregnant at the time she disappeared.

A week later, on April 2, a road-paving crew saw a body below a Waipahu freeway overpass near Waikele Stream. When the police examined the body, they found that it was Louise Medeiros, wearing only the red-and-white flowered blouse she had on when she got on the plane on Kaua'i.

Again, the victim's hands were tied behind her back.

By this time, fear stalked the community. People joked nervously to women who even vaguely met the profile of the victim: young, Caucasian-looking and in the wrong place at the wrong time. Policewomen who resembled the victims were being placed as decoys in the airport–Ke'ehi Lagoon area. Despite all this, another woman died.

The fifth victim was Linda Pesce, a thirty-six-year-old sales representative for McCaw Telepage in Kaka'ako. Linda left work at about 6:30 P.M. on Tuesday, April 29, after learning that she had been promoted in her job. She was wearing a light-blue turtleneck dress, a white cotton jacket, and white high heels.

Her roommate reported the brown-haired woman missing on Wednesday morning when she failed to come home. Police found her car that afternoon, parked near the Nimitz Highway viaduct leading to the H-1 Freeway, near the airport. Witnesses told police they saw the car parked on the roadside with its emergency flashers on at about 7:00 on Tuesday night.

Family and friends described Linda as a bold, strong person with an unconventional past. Originally from Marin County, California, she left college in the 1970s to strike out on adventures. She hitch-hiked across the country by herself, flew to Honolulu and worked as a dancer in a nightclub, moved to Guam and danced in other clubs, and then moved back to Hawai'i.

Friends described Linda, who was 5 feet 4 inches tall and weighed 146 pounds, as tough and streetwise, quick with an opinion and fearless. But they also said she became much more conventional and less wild after the birth of her daughter, seven years before.

Four days after she got word of her promotion, some people who had gone looking for friends who were fishing for squid discovered Linda's nude body. Again, the victim's hands were tied behind her back.

By this time, the entire community was on alert. Gun sales shot up. Women signed up for self-defense classes. Police gave tips to community groups across the island. A coalition of women's groups provided advice and warnings to women on ways to protect themselves. Hundreds of people telephoned the police, keeping the twenty-seven-member police task force jumping.

One of the problems within the task force was that two lieutenants had equal authority and command over the investigators. This was a crucial management mistake: two people should never be put in charge of one task. It violates the managerial concept of "unity of command," which states that employees have but one supervisor to answer to, one supervisor to take instructions from. This dual command within the task force proved difficult, with one lieutenant issuing one set of orders and the other issuing another that countermanded the first. The officers of the task force felt the conflict daily. The arguments over what course of action to take were sometimes loud and took a toll on the task force members, all of whom felt pressured to succeed quickly.

⊕

One of the key investigators into the serial killings remains convinced that police arrested the right man. Police major Louis Souza was one of the lieutenants assigned to the case. He says the deaths of the five women weigh on his mind "every day," even though more than fifteen years have passed. He noted that the abductions occurred and all the bodies were found in or near the route between 'Ewa Beach, where the suspect lived, and an air cargo company near the airport on Lagoon Drive, where he worked.

Souza said the suspect went to Honolulu police on his own and claimed that a psychic told him where to find Linda Pesce's body. The suspect knew Linda; she had been trying to sell him a pager. Police found his name written in work notes that Linda left behind.

"He came forward to the police and said that he saw some bones or a body in Sand Island," Souza said. The suspect took the police to Sand Island. Once there, they looked all over the place, but he stayed away from the exact place where the body was dumped. Her body was later found 150 yards from the place he took them.

Souza has spent a lot of time thinking about the killings and the man police arrested. Souza said the suspect's ex-wife and girlfriends painted him as a smooth talker. "Before you know it, he'd be talking to you about sex."

They also told investigators that the man used to tie them up with their hands behind their back to have sex, in a manner identical to the way the murder victims were found.

By the time police issued the bulletin that they were looking for a van with writing on the back, Souza said, "we were already watching him." In fact, he said police watched as the suspect scratched his company insignia off the back of the van.

The first big public break in the case came when witnesses said they had seen a light-colored cargo van parked near Linda's car when it was stopped along the road. Police set up roadblocks and talked to others who traveled that road regularly at the same hour, looking for people who might have seen the killer. People described a Caucasian man or one of mixed ancestry, medium build, in his late thirties or early forties.

Police also weren't saying that they had another clue. The sex-assault aspect of the crime left evidence of semen with few or no sperm, likely from someone who had had a vasectomy.

The FBI's Behavioral Science Unit, which studies serial killings, produced a profile of what Honolulu's killer might be like. Then-Honolulu Police Chief Doug Gibb held a news conference to describe the killer's likely characteristics. Gibb told reporters that the murderer was apt to be "an opportunist," striking available victims, rather than someone who was stalking a certain type of person. He said the man probably committed the crimes in an area that he knows, so police speculated that he lived or worked in the area between Sand Island and Waipahu, where four of the women appeared to have been picked up and where all five bodies were found. He also predicted the man would not have a criminal record and that he might be someone who was having marital problems or disagreements with a girlfriend.

Police Major Hughes also told reporters that evidence in one of the five cases wasn't as convincingly connected as the others. But following classic police custom, he declined to say which one. Investigators later said there were elements of the Medeiros killing that didn't fit the established pattern. For example, her body was found wrapped with much more tape than the other victims.

Six days after Linda's body was found—on May 9—police arrested a 43-year-old Caucasian man on suspicion of killing her. Souza remembers the night of the arrest in great detail. "He came in voluntarily. But he came in late. It was about eight o'clock in the evening when we started talking to him."

The suspect allowed police to photograph him and give him a polygraph examination, which Souza said he failed. Souza watched two detectives interrogate him through the glass and he said the suspect's body language showed the telltale signs associated with guilt: arms crossed, head down, defensive.

After several hours, Souza had seen enough. "It was about three o'clock in the morning. I went into the interview room and said, 'If he says he's tired, we should stop,' because the interview would be tainted."

When you interview someone, common sense plays a big role in what can occur legally. That means no physical force and no psychological manipulation. That also means police cannot do what is considered "inherent coercion" such as not allowing people to have water, food, or sleep, or interviewing them under blinding light.

Souza also confronted the suspect about Pesce's death. What if a detective accused you of killing someone you knew? What would you say? Souza said the suspect at first didn't deny the murder. "All he did was put his head down and cross his hands across his chest." Then, softly, he said he didn't do it, Souza recalls.

Souza told the detectives to arrest him. "I believed there was enough probable cause to arrest him." While the interview was going on, the suspect's girlfriend had called a woman friend who was an attorney. When the detectives took a break in the interview, the suspect was held by the Receiving Desk, routinely staffed with inexperienced officers.

To this day, Souza believes that the suspect was on the brink of breaking and telling police what had happened. "We let him rest, and while he was in the cellblock, [the attorney] called in to the cellblock. Our recruits back there in the cellblock, they don't know any different, so they allowed her to speak to him," Souza said.

"She told him, 'I've been retained by your girlfriend so I don't want you to talk to the police any more.'" Souza sees the rookie mistake of allowing the intervention of an attorney as a crucial one. "If he wanted to talk to somebody, he could use the phone. But we have no obligation to honor an incoming call."

Ten hours after he walked in the door, the suspect was released from police custody. Once the suspect stopped talking, police turned to prosecutors with that they had. Prosecutors told Souza there wasn't enough to charge the suspect with the murder.

Souza remembers watching the suspect walk out of the basement offices of the old Pāwaʻa police station, up to Young Street. With TV cameras rolling, reporters asked Souza: "You think the police got the right man?" Souza ruefully recalls his reply as "Yeah."

So, what happened to the case? Souza said prosecutors were reluctant to take the case to trial without more evidence linking the suspect to all the killings. "We gathered a lot of information on the fifth one. But the prosecutors were very skeptical of going on that one because they wanted to try all five."

Even after the prosecutors declined to go forward with initial charges, police remained confident they had found the right man and continued to gather evidence. About two months after his arrest, police located a woman who said she had seen a man with Pesce on the night of the murder. The witness said she hadn't talked to police earlier because she was afraid the suspect could recognize her. "She didn't want to come forward," Souza said, but when she did "she picked him out from a photo lineup."

There were other reasons the case didn't go anywhere. One was a personality clash police had with the prosecutors on that case and others. Souza said he and the other lieutenant had spent two days arguing with the prosecutors over how they should proceed on their search warrant.

When prosecutors resisted, Souza said the lieutenants went around the lawyers and took their case directly to a judge to issue the search warrant. The procedure to obtain a warrant is linked directly to the Fourth Amendment, which requires the review of a magistrate. Detectives discuss search warrants with prosecutors as a courtesy, not as a legal requirement. The practice, however, has been in place for so long that it is difficult to move around it. Prosecutors expect to be included in discussions before detectives confer with a judge. When detectives bypass that discussion, a very definite conflict erupts between police and prosecutors. "So we went and we searched, but we didn't find anything. Under his house, his cars, everything, his van, his workplace, down at the airport," Souza said.

Police had hoped the search would link the killings through personal items taken from the victims but they didn't find such evidence. Still, Souza stands behind the decision to search. "The prosecutor don't tell me how to work my case. I don't tell him how to prosecute."

Another problem with the case from the prosecution's view was the witness descriptions. Police ended up with five or six very different composite drawings of the suspect. Souza says he believes the confusion came from witnesses and police officers who were trying too hard. Investigators turned up about a dozen witnesses, who were interviewed by police about what they saw the night of Pesce's disappearance. "The officers, in the manner of trying to see what they could do, kind of intimidated the witnesses," Souza said. "So what the witnesses did was, they gave descriptions of relatives or whoever, just to get the officers off their back." Souza said the witnesses saw something, but not enough for them all to agree on a suspect description. "We had a lot of probable cause, enough circumstantial evidence to say that it was him."

Police believed they'd found another key bit of evidence when the girlfriend indicated that the suspect sometimes went off on his own after the two got into arguments that coincided with the killings. "He'd end up going out on the prowl," Souza said, which left the task force feeling that they had discovered the trigger for the killings.

Even though the suspect was never charged, Souza says he thinks the community relaxed again after the arrest. "They felt confident again that this type of thing would probably not happen again, with the same guy anyway."

The suspect's release gave police a new responsibility. The evidence pointed to him. The police believed that he was the killer. But now, the police were returning him to the community. Many people—investigators, psychologists, and social scientists—believe that serial killers cannot be rehabilitated. Some people also believe that the killers' motivation is so great that they continue to kill under the most threatening of circumstances. And HPD could not, with any conscience at all, release the man they believed to be a serial killer back into the community without watching him.

So the members of the task force took on a new chore: tailing him, tracking his movements. The police were close to him around the clock at his home and business. Wherever he went, HPD officers went. When he went on trips to the mainland, so did the police. When he left the state, HPD notified the police in the city to which he moved.

At the time, the daily newspapers and several of the television stations followed a policy of not naming people who were arrested unless they were charged. This case was so high-profile for the community that several news organizations broke from the policy and named him. (Because arrest information is public record, the media did nothing wrong.)

For weeks after the arrest, the community focused on the killings. A group of fifteen businesses and other organizations helped put together a $25,000 reward for information leading to an arrest and indictment in connection with the unsolved murders of the five women. No one ever collected the reward.

Police continue to keep track of the suspect and other suspects in high-profile crimes through the FBI's ViCAP national clearinghouse of information. The Violent Criminal Apprehension Program collects and analyzes characteristics of murders to help law enforcement find the killers.

As of 2002, the Honolulu suspect lived in the Midwest, according to Souza. "He went to Amsterdam a couple of times, he's been to the East Coast, he's passed through here," but he hasn't been linked to any other murders since, here or in another city. "Anytime there are similar cases, they immediately start to look where he's at," Souza said.

Souza said he waits for word of the suspect, wondering if there will be a break in the case, wondering how long the man will live. Even now, he perks up when he hears word of a new interview with a witness, looking for clues that might officially end the mystery. "Still, 'til today, this was the guy. I got no doubt. Because as soon as he left, it stopped."

People can take precautions in their daily lives to avoid some dangers. Although tips on personal security are certainly no guarantee of safety, they can help.

• It's safer to travel with others than alone.

• When you do need to go someplace alone, tell a friend or relative where you are going, how you will get there, and when you expect to arrive.

• Carry a whistle or other noisemaker. Or just yell if you sense trouble.

• Keep your car in good working order. Buy flares and use them. If your car does break down, use an emergency phone. Get out of the car only to set up the flares and open the hood. Get back in the car, lock the doors and leave the windows open only enough for ventilation.

• Don't accept a ride from a stranger, no matter what. That includes a taxi you didn't call or official-looking vehicles with only one police officer present.

• While waiting for a bus or car or walking along the street, stand back from the curb so that you cannot be easily pulled into a car and dragged away.

- Be aware of your surroundings. If a car passes and returns while you are waiting, be wary. As you walk to your car alone, hold your keys in your hand so you can quickly enter your car and drive away.

- If you think something is wrong, it probably is. Your own intuition is sometimes the best advice.

- Walk facing traffic so you can see vehicles approaching.

- Walk in the center of the sidewalk and pay attention to brush and bushes where people may hide.

- If you're walking and you notice you're being followed, walk to where people are. If you're driving and you're being followed, drive to a gas station or a police station or somewhere there are other people and call the police.

John Douglas, Robert Ressler, and Ann Burgess, in their book *Sexual Homicide: Patterns and Motives,* suggest that once a serial killer has selected his victim and launched his fatal fantasy, there is little that victim can do to escape his assault if she allows herself to be vulnerable. Cases have shown that serial killers prefer victims who are vulnerable.

The best approach a woman can take is to reduce her risk factor by avoiding circumstances that make it easy for a serial killer to select her as his victim. Don't hitchhike, for example. When a woman reduces her vulnerability, she increases the risk the serial killer must take to make her his victim. A serial killer who takes a victim walking along a dark, lonely, and secluded roadway has a low risk versus one who takes a potential victim from a crowded mall parking lot.

The FBI has stated many times that there isn't a major city in the United States that has escaped being terrorized by a serial killer. Even Honolulu.

8

Mass Murder: The Touchette and Dela Cruz Families

I was asleep when the pager went off. A few minutes later I was on the telephone with the night-shift lieutenant.

"Sorry to wake you, but we have a house fire in Kailua where two children were killed and two adults are in critical condition."

"Okay, I'm on my way."

The death of children eats at most of us like no other crime. Usually they are the most innocent of victims, with no means of defending themselves, often killed by adults who try to justify their fatal abuse by blaming the children. These killers wrap themselves in a blanket of self-preservation when they get caught and deflect blame from themselves to innocent children. "Why should I be punished because the kid died. I didn't mean for the kid to die. If the kid had only behaved. After all, it was only a kid." This type of killer makes most of us investigators work even harder to ensure we conduct a complete and thorough investigation.

I was bracing myself for a different kind of death investigation as I drove out to the Kailua scene. A house fire. An accident. Perhaps the result of faulty wiring or a careless cigarette. Either way, two children, Kalah and Joshua Touchette, were dead, The thought that they might have suffered started to work on my mind. By the time I got there I was already tense. And the sight of the fire trucks and hoses and ambulances and police cars with flashing blue lights caused my stomach to tighten further. I saw one of my detectives walking with a uniformed officer, and I parked my car to join them.

"Lieutenant, we just learned from HFD (Honolulu Fire Department) that they suspect the fire was started deliberately,

This was not an accident. We have a double murder of the children, and there's a possibility that the parents might die as well."

I felt the anger growing as I walked with the detective around the house and he briefed me on what he already knew. Based on the evidence at the scene and partial statements from the mother of the children, it appeared that someone broke into the house and set it on fire. There was very little information at this early stage, but the HFD preliminary report indicated that an accelerant had been used to start the fire. The firefighters who put out the fire could smell gasoline.

The firefighters still had control of the crime scene, and our investigation was in its earliest stages when my pager went off again. It was the graveyard-shift lieutenant's number.

"Dias, we have another case. A double murder in Waipahu."

It seemed the most inopportune time to leave the scene of the arson. Arson is a crime that is complicated by possible destruction of evidence by the fire, the addition of tons of water, and firefighters moving throughout the scene. It creates a contamination factor that is extraordinarily difficult to overcome. But in spite of the fire and water damage, three basic questions in an arson case must be answered: Where did the fire start? How did the fire start? Was the fire started deliberately?

Arson investigators look for signs that indicate a fire was deliberately started. This means they must locate the origin of the fire. There are several signs they look for:

• Alligatoring: This is the checkered blister pattern on the surface of wood caused by heat or burning. An intense alligatoring pattern is an indication of point of origin.

• Depth of char: The deepest char is often found at the point of origin.

• Pour pattern: When an accelerant such as gasoline is poured across a surface, a discernible pattern occurs, which often outlines the edges of the spill.

• Inverted cone, or V pattern: This indicates that the fire started at a particular location and burned upward and outward, creating a V pattern indicating the origin of the fire at the apex of the V.

• Spalling: When a concrete floor chips due to stress from a burning accelerant, this indicates point of origin.

One other tool in an arson investigation that people forget is the human nose. Many accelerants have recognizable odors, and experienced firefighters can recognize the smell of gasoline, kerosene, or other flammable substances. This is not a perfect method of determining arson, but it is a method that should not be ignored, especially when other evidence has gone up in flames.

To identify the accelerant, char evidence must be collected and preserved. The char evidence is placed into an airtight container and preserved for later laboratory examination. A gas chromatograph/mass spectrometer is used to analyze the suspected accelerant. A graph is produced and compared with known samples. The final result identifying the substance is often very specific.

In arson cases in which death has occurred, an autopsy may determine whether the person died as a result of smoke inhalation or burns from the fire or was dead prior to the fire. Most fires spread rapidly over a few minutes and produce toxic smoke. In most fire deaths, the victim dies as a result of smoke inhalation rather than burning. In an autopsy, the pathologist examines the throat and lungs. If smoke and soot residue is not present, the indication is that the person died before inhaling the smoke, or was dead before the fire started. The presence of soot and smoke residue indicates the victim was alive and breathing during the course of the fire.

In a death by fire, the muscles tighten and contract as a result of the heat. This causes the victim's fingers, arms, and legs to move to a position resembling that of a boxer or prize fighter. This is known as the "pugilistic condition."

When children are involved in fire cases, rescuers must look for them under beds or in closets or other locations where children will hide from the smoke and flame. Every family should discuss evacuation routes and what children should do in the event of a fire.

On April 3, 1988, investigators were called to a fire death in Wai'anae along a dirt road to the rear of a row of houses. In the early morning hours, one of the residents smelled smoke, and when he looked, he saw a vehicle burning. The neighbor called 911 for the Honolulu Fire Department and ran out to the car. By the time he got there, the flames were gone but the interior was filled with smoke. Looking through the glass, he could see a man sitting upright in the driver's seat. When he opened the door it was obvious that the man, later identified as thirty-one-year-old Lorenzo Young, was dead.

Firefighters arrived and extinguished the smoldering fire. They checked Young for signs of life but could tell from their experience that he was dead. The victim suffered damage to his ears, and his body was stiff as a result of the intense heat. One of his hands was on his lap, on top of material from the car's ceiling, an indication that the pugilistic condition had occurred. His arm moved after the material from the ceiling had fallen to his lap. In addition, Young's head was in a full upright position. The homicide detail was called, and a murder investigation begun.

Examination of the interior of the vehicle revealed that the killer or killers had used some of Young's IRS tax preparation forms soaked in an accellerant as fuel. The five-gallon gasoline can was found among the springs of the passenger side of the front seat. The plastic and foam of the seat had burned away, and the can had fallen through into the springs and wires of the seat.

When he started the fire, however, the killer shut the door with the windows up. This created a closed system, and the fire quickly used up the oxygen inside the car. With the oxygen gone, the fire extinguished itself. Fire, also known as "combustion," requires three things to continue: oxygen, fuel, and a source of heat. Remove either one of the three and combustion cannot continue.

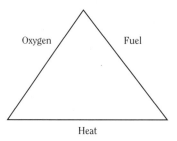

After examining and processing the interior of the car, attendants from the morgue removed Young's body. When they did, several firearm shell casings fell out of the car; however, we could not detect any injuries other than the damage to his ears.

An autopsy conducted the following day showed that Young had been shot several times in the back of his head. His throat and lungs were completely clear of soot, which indicated that he was killed prior to the fire. A check into Young's past showed that he was associated with a suspected drug dealer, and when his friends were interviewed, they told investigators that he owed that dealer lots of money for drugs already used. The investigation at the time identified another Wai'anae resident, Dido Rodrigues, who, years later, was arrested and convicted of Young's murder and sentenced to life in prison.

With very little traffic on the roadway, my drive to Waipahu was a quick one. I would soon learn however, that this second scene was really the first.

The Waipahu scene was not as chaotic as the Kailua scene, but there were still a large number of neighborhood onlookers. The house had two stories, with the main living area upstairs. By the time I arrived at the scene, several hours had passed, and the processing was well under way. The lead detective briefed me on the information he got from the suspect's wife.

The mug photograph of Orlando Ganal

Orlando and Mabel Ganal were separated. She lived at the scene with her parents and their teen-aged son. Orlando lived in the home they owned together at another subdivision in Waipahu. The couple were separated because Mabel had been seeing another man. She had confessed this to Orlando and left him to go and live with her parents.

Mabel was dating a man who had moved to the islands from the mainland. When they first met, he was staying with his brother and the brother's family on Oʻahu. By that terrible night, he had moved to his own place. Mabel admitted that, in the arguments she had with Orlando, she had taunted him about her lover, and it only served to make Orlando even more angry.

On the night of the killings, August 25, 1991, Orlando drove to his in-laws' home armed with a .357-magnum revolver. He climbed the outside stairs to the front door, but found it locked. He demanded entry but was refused. This enraged him even more, and he kicked the door in, injuring his foot. The first person to confront him was his mother-in-law, Aradina Dela Cruz. Ganal shot her in the mouth as she tried to block him from entering the house. She died instantly, falling onto the living-room couch.

Mabel ran down the hall to the stairwell at the rear of the house. She knew her husband would kill her, and her only opportunity to survive was to flee. Orlando fired several rounds at her as she ran, but Mabel was able to run out of the house and hide in a neighbor's yard several houses away.

In the moments after the first shot was fired, Ganal's father-in-law,

Santiago Dela Cruz, came out of the bedroom. He was shot as soon as he confronted Ganal. Now in a complete rage, Ganal shot his own teenaged son, Orlando Jr., when the boy stepped into the hall.

The mortally injured father-in-law struggled back into the bedroom and called for police and an ambulance. With people lying dead, badly wounded, and dying about him, Ganal stopped and reloaded his gun. The weapon, a revolver, required Ganal to open the cylinder, remove the spent shell casings and reload. In doing this, he dropped a .357 magnum cartridge on the floor. This piece of evidence would become important later to show that Ganal was indeed the suspect at both scenes.

Realizing that Mabel was gone, Orlando left the house and drove away before patrol officers arrived.

He had failed to kill his wife, but in his wake he left his murdered mother-in-law, his wounded father-in-law, who would die later at the hospital, and his critically injured son. But his murderous rage had not yet subsided.

Information we had from both scenes soon made it apparent that the suspect in the Kailua arson was also Orlando Ganal. We confirmed this when Mabel told us that she was seeing a man named Touchette, who had stayed with his brother in Kailua. The family in the burned home was named Touchette. We now believed that Orlando Ganal was responsible for the murders of the two children in Kailua and the critical injuries inflicted on their parents.

Our reconstruction showed that when Ganal left Waipahu, he drove to Kailua, where he stopped at an all-night service station. There, he filled a five-gallon can with gasoline. His next stop was the Touchette home, off Oneawa Street. We're not exactly sure what happened next, but somehow, a spent .357-shell casing, probably from one of the bullets fired at the Waipahu murder scene, fell from his truck onto the roadway. It lay there until it was run over or stepped on as the firefighters arrived.

Ganal then entered the residence of Michael and Wendy Touchette as they slept. He poured the gasoline around the living

Orlando Ganal pouring gasoline in the Touchette home

room, the hallway, and the bedrooms where the Touchettes and their two young children lay sleeping. Then in an act of cowardly bravado, he woke the Touchettes, shouting of his revenge. As he ran from the house, he lit the gasoline, causing the house to burst into flames.

Wendy and Michael ran through the flames, desperately trying to get to their children. But the fire was too intense. It burned their hands, their faces, their bodies. They lost their way in the fire and were forced to run from the house, both engulfed in flames. Their children died that night, lying in their beds.

The coward Ganal drove back to his own house, where police officers arrested him. Ganal was dressed only in his underwear. He told the officers that he went to the beach to wash himself. And he wanted a doctor because he had a cut on his foot. And it hurt. After all the pain and suffering that he had inflicted that night, he complained because his foot hurt.

Orlando Ganal was tried and convicted of murder in the first degree, the most serious grade of murder in the state of Hawai'i, reserved for the most heinous of killers. At the trial, Mabel Ganal professed her love for the man who murdered her parents. She professed her love for the man who murdered two innocent children and their father. And she professed her love for the man who nearly murdered her son, and who maimed and disfigured the mother of the murdered children. She later moved to the mainland with David Touchette, the lover that Ganal had sought to kill.

The two people Ganal had targeted in his anger escaped injury. The Touchette children and their father died; their mother was devastated, severely burned over 40 percent of her body and scarred forever. Their only crime? Providing a place to stay for Michael Touchette's brother at a time when he got together with the wrong woman. Mabel Ganal's parents, Santiago and Aradina Dela Cruz, were also dead. Their crime? Taking in their own daughter and grandson during a stressful time in their lives.

9
Murdered Children: Satoshi Komiya, Michael Chun, and Pauline Rodrigues

Ask investigators what crime really gets to them and you'll find one category that universally pierces their professional façade—adults who abuse or murder children. Children are the most vulnerable of all victims. Even investigators who don't have kids or don't particularly care for them remember life as a child and how much their parents meant to them. Children depend on adults for their well-being and safety. They can't fight back. Even under the most abusive situations, children will return to abusive parents; after all, they're the only parents they know. And yet, it is usually the parents who cause children the most pain.

On June 20, 2001, the nation was shocked when it learned of the Texas mother, Andrea Yates, who drowned her five children, one after another. Yates was a Christian mom who home-schooled her children, all of whom had names drawn from the Bible. She drowned her three younger sons first: five-year-old John, three-year-old Paul, and two-year-old Luke. While she was drowning her six-month-old daughter, Mary, her seven-year-old son, Noah, walked in on her. After chasing him through the house, she dragged him back to the bathroom and drowned him.

In court, Yates pleaded not guilty by reason of insanity. Some expert witnesses claimed she suffered from postpartum depression. The jury rejected that claim, believing that to drown her older children required strength and purpose beyond that of a depressed person. She was found guilty and sentenced to life in prison.

Her husband reported that he still cared for her in spite of the terrible tragedy. Many people wondered why he had not seen any warning signs that his wife was in trouble.

This nationally publicized case of a mother drowning her children was shocking, but was not the first such case. More than thirty-five years ago, an 'Aiea woman drowned her five children in the bathtub in a case that bears an eerie similarity to that of Andrea Yates.

On November 22, 1965, Honolulu police reported that Maggie Lee Young, the thirty-eight-year-old wife of an Air Force captain, killed her five children at their home on Nalopaka Place. The children who died were Frankie, who was eight; Janice, five; Judith, three; Jeannette, nearly two; and Jessica, seven months.

According to news accounts of the time, Young had been hospitalized early that year after suffering a nervous breakdown, and she repeatedly told family and friends that she thought she was not a good enough mother for the children.

On the morning of November 22, she told police she drowned the girls one by one—from the oldest to the youngest—after her son left for Alvah Scott Elementary School about eight o'clock. Then she went to the school, picked him up at about 9:30, and also drowned him in the bathtub. She laid the children out on their beds as if preparing them to go to sleep. Three court-appointed psychiatrists found Young to be mentally unbalanced when she murdered her children.

Then-Circuit Judge Samuel P. King ruled that she was insane and committed her to the Hawai'i State Hospital in Kāne'ohe on January 31, 1966. About six months later—while on a pass that allowed her freedom within the hospital campus—she walked into a chicken slaughterhouse on the grounds of the hospital and hanged herself from the rafters.

On Saturday, July 24, 1966, hospital officials initially reported that she had escaped. The police issued alerts. While police searched the community, hospital officials failed to look very closely at their own property. Soon, however, it became clear that she had not gone very far. Her body was discovered two days later when farm workers opened the building as they arrived for work on Monday morning.

Hospital officials said at the time that she had been progressing in group-therapy sessions and was growing more aware of what she had done to her five young children. A doctor at the time said, "She was beginning to realize the enormity of it."

Cases of mothers who murder their children during periods of depression are reported from time to time in the United States. Often, like Andrea Yates, the women say that they were not good enough mothers. But murdering your children because you made a mistake on some travel arrangements? Maybe in an earlier century. Or another culture. And at least in one instance in Waikīkī.

On August 15, 1988, Mariko Komiya, her husband, Takeya, and their three children flew to Hawai'i with other tourists from Osaka, Japan. Mariko Komiya was in charge of travel arrangements for a third of the group of thirty. Three days into their vacation, a tour representative visited Mariko's room at the Hilton Hawaiian Village Hotel late that evening to notify the Komiyas that an error had been made and there were only nine return tickets, one short of what was needed for all ten tourists to return home to Japan. Mariko Komiya got very upset about the mistake, even though the travel agent assured her that the arrangements could be worked out so that everyone could return home together. Her husband told her to go to sleep and not worry about it. He returned to his nearby room while she remained in room 768 with their three sons. Then, a terrible plan apparently began to form in her mind.

First, she wrote a suicide note, which she left on the dresser. Then she prepared to have her children join her in death: her oldest son, sixteen-year-old Naomichi, who was mentally retarded; ten-year-old Hirouki; and four-year-old Satoshi. She tied two pairs of pants together and used them to strap her youngest to her back. Then she tried to push Naomichi over the railing of the hotel balcony, but he struggled to get away and ran back into the room. She picked up Hirouki and threw him over the rail. Then she climbed

Mariko Komiya leaping to her death with son Satoshi strapped to her back

over the railing, with Satoshi sleeping on her back, and jumped seven stories to the flagstone sidewalk below. She died on impact, and the boy died hours later at The Queen's Medical Center.

Hirouki escaped death that night. Later, he told police that he remembered his mother taking him and his brothers out onto the hotel lanai, being sleepy, and then having the sensation of falling before grabbing onto something.

Hirouki got some help that night from another visitor, thirty-six-year-old Don Garrison, a native of Whittier, California, who was sleeping in the room next door. Garrison was awakened by people in the street below screaming, "She's dead!" He rushed to the lanai, saw a body sprawled on the ground, and then saw a little boy hanging from the outside of the balcony railing next door. Without thought for his own safety, Garrison climbed from his balcony to theirs, risking his own life as he worked to rescue the little boy, who was screaming in Japanese. When Garrison reached the Komiyas' balcony, he leaned over the rail and pulled Hirouki from where he was dangling, back to safety. The boy hugged him and said "thank you" in English.

Meanwhile, another visitor—Shoichiro Matsumura, from Kochi, Japan—heard Hirouki's screams from his ninth-floor room, looked out and saw him hanging from the rail and rushed down to the room to help. There, he ran into Takeya Komiya, struggling to get into the room where his family was, but having trouble getting the key into the lock to open it.

Matsumura followed the distraught dad into the hotel room. He later told police that Hirouki told them his mother had fallen. Upon hearing this, Matsumura said he tried to comfort the boy. He told Takeya to go downstairs to try to help his wife, while he stayed with the two boys and Garrison.

In most suicides, people who kill themselves don't leave notes. But in this case, Mariko Komiya offered her own explanation of the tragedy, in a brief letter written on hotel stationery and addressed to her mother.

Translated by police, the letter read:

Dear Mom,
I'm sorry I'm going before you. Please be happy I'm going before you. If people found out the things I had done, they won't be in doubt I can't live in this world any longer. I causedmany, many inconveniences to you it is natural I'm doing this.

From your child.

I'm very sorry to cause trouble to people working for the hotel. Please take care of the things after I left. I want you to bury my ashes in this island.

Maybe it is not possible because I am not American.

Later, Takeya told investigators that she had a strange look on her face when they parted. Only after it was too late did he realize the significance of her expression.

In Japanese culture, when people believe they have done a terribly bad thing, something that has brought shame to themselves and their family, ritual suicide is a way of atoning for this weakness. In some instances, Japanese women will also kill their children as part of this atonement. To leave them behind after bringing more shame on their family would amount to abandonment.

In that woman's mind, she was atoning for her shameful act by killing herself and her children. In today's world, where ancient cultural acts of ritual suicide are frowned upon, her actions are unthinkable.

Mariko Komiya's actions were not typical of the child abuse that investigators see. She simply murdered her child. But the death of Michael Chun was caused by continued child abuse—mental abuse, physical abuse, and malnutrition—over a long period of time. Unlike Satoshi Komiya, whose death took but a few seconds, Michael Chun took a very long time to die. And he probably died feeling unwanted and alone.

Michael Chun lived in Wai'anae with his mother and stepfather. Witnesses described Michael as an active boy. He was normal for a child of his age—except for being the target of repeated physical abuse. His mother told police that on August 2, 1986, Michael slipped and fell and crashed into a patio table. On August 5, Michael began to act funny. He said his stomach hurt, he acted dizzy, and he started to vomit. Later that night he became unconscious. His mother took him to Wai'anae Comprehensive Clinic. From there he was evacuated by air to Kuakini Medical Center, and at 8:30 in the morning on August 6, 1986, Michael Chun died.

Examination of his body revealed many small bruises of varying ages, covering his entire body. There were larger bruises to his eyes and torso and stomach. Some were old and faded, some were black, and some were bluish purple. Doctors found that the skin on the inside of his lips was cut and torn, as if he had been punched in the mouth. The skin behind his ears—where the ears meet the skull— were ripped and jaggedly torn, suggesting that his ears were pulled with great force.

When questioned, Michael's mother, Michelle Cabral, said that Michael's two-year-old stepbrother hit him with a small stick, causing the bruises. She explained his stomach injury as having occurred when Michael, who was running, fell against the patio table. She did not know what caused his other injuries.

The investigation showed that Michael Chun died of medical neglect and child abuse. Michelle Cabral amended her statement. She acknowledged that her husband, Clifford Cabral, didn't like Michael because he was the son of another man. She now accused Clifford of hitting Michael with a stick.

The efforts by Clifford and Michelle Cabral to blame Michael's death on his running into a table were not believed by the jury hearing their case. They were both convicted of murder.

People who suspect a child of being abused should report their suspicions to the police. There are tell-tale signs of abuse. Look for multiple bruises of varying ages and degrees. Some are new and red, some are middle-aged and blue or black, and some are old and nearly faded away. Parents use the excuse, "Oh, she's always bumping into things." Look on the arms. The inner arms will show four bruises in a row and a corresponding single bruise on the outside of the arm. This is where the child has been grabbed.

Look inside the mouth, inside the lips. Abusive parents tend to hit their children in the mouth. Teeth cut the inner lips, and when the swelling goes down, the tears of the inner lip remain. Look behind the ears. There may be a tearing of the skin where the ear meets the skull. This occurs when the abuser pulls on the ear much too hard and rips the skin.

Look for the very thin child. The child who looks sickly may be malnourished.

Look for these injuries in a child who you suspect is being abused. If you find them, call the police. Speak for the child who has no voice. Others can reach out to care—relatives who may be far away and unaware, friends or foster families willing to offer a fresh start at a normal life.

Michael Chun had all the classic child abuse injuries. Michael Chun was four years old when he died. More accurately, Michael Chun was four years old when he was murdered.

Occasionally the media reports a missing child or teen whose body is later discovered. Across the nation, young children have been taken from their bedrooms, from their schools and playgrounds. Older children, too, are abducted, sometimes when they place themselves in dangerous situations.

Pauline Rodrigues was a sixteen-year-old from Maui. In September 1987 she was living with her aunt in Waipi'o Gentry while her parents were going through a divorce. Pauline was a normal young girl who was at the age of self-confidence and self-reliance, a factor that perhaps created a false sense of security. She may have overestimated her ability to provide for her own safety.

Each school morning she walked from her aunt's home to the

bus stop on Kamehameha Highway. She rode the bus to the intersection of Kamehameha Highway and Waimano Home Road in Pearl City. There she walked a little way up the hill to the next bus stop, where she boarded another bus for the remainder of the trip to Pearl City High School. This second bus stop was directly across the street from the Pearl City Police Station.

It was a Monday morning around seven o'clock. Pauline was waiting at the second bus stop. It was change of shift at Pearl City Police Department. About twenty-five police officers were going on and coming off duty. While Pauline was waiting, a white pick-up truck pulled up near the service station behind the bus stop. Her friends later told police that the driver of the truck offered a ride to the group of girls at the bus stop. Pauline was the only one who got into the truck. That was the last time they saw her alive.

Pauline's aunt reported her missing later that evening. Pauline never made it to school, and no one had any idea as to her whereabouts. The Missing Persons Detail was given a school picture of Pauline and checked with her friends, with no luck. Four days later, on Friday afternoon, a fisherman driving on a dirt road in Hau Bush in ʻEwa Beach noticed a foul odor coming from a garbage dump as he slowly maneuvered the rutted, gouged-out road. He was curious and stopped. Then he saw what he feared: the nude body of a woman lying among the garbage.

Arriving officers called for the Homicide Detail. It was late Friday afternoon, so I notified the next team of the murder. One of the detectives said he couldn't come because he was an assistant coach for a local private school and needed to be at a football game. I informed him that his job came before the game and that I did not approve his time off to attend the game. He chose the game. I called another detective, and the football coach was later disciplined and transferred from the detail.

That man had real problems with his priorities. The investigation of a murder had become for him just another case. He no longer felt the deep conviction that he was entrusted with the grave responsibility of finding the person who took the life of someone's child or parent or brother or sister. To abandon his partner and responsibilities was, in my mind, a statement that he no longer belonged in the Homicide Detail. I transferred that detective with a clear conscience.

When the investigating team arrived at the scene, we moved carefully through the garbage dump, searching for items that might be related to this murder. The woman's body was partially covered with some burned planks of wood. That, together with the dark brown and black discoloration of her skin, led us to initially believe that someone tried to burn her body—perhaps to hide her identification. This proved inaccurate. Her body discoloration was the result of decomposition in the hot sun of 'Ewa Beach.

We thought the killer might have left tire-track impressions somewhere in the dirt along that unpaved road, or just off the road near the garbage dump. Carefully we tried to locate and not disturb any impression evidence.

Impression evidence takes many forms, from shoe- and footprints to tire tracks to tool marks to human and animal bites. Such marks are classified into two types: compression evidence, when the impression is made by pushing or by pressure; and scraping marks, made with a combination of compression and sliding. This type of evidence can be photographed or castings of the impression can be made. To cast an impression of a footprint or tire track, we start by building a frame to encase the area that we're going to cast, much the same way you might frame an area where you're going to pour concrete. The casting material is usually plaster of paris, which, like concrete, is heavy and could damage the fine details of the impressions. To keep the fine ridge detail intact, we spray the print or track with hairspray, allow it to dry, and spray it again several times, allowing each coat to dry. This forms a hard coating that helps to protect the impression from the heavy casting material. The plaster of paris is mixed with water, and a thin layer is poured into the frame around the print. Before it dries, a layer of gauze is placed on the wet plaster. Another layer is poured and another layer of gauze is applied. This is done three or four times, depending on the size of the cast. The gauze acts as a stabilizing agent to prevent the cast from cracking, the way wire does in concrete. The cast is allowed to dry in place, the frame is removed, and the casting is picked up. Any dirt or sand that clings to it can be brushed away, revealing a reverse impression of the original print or track.

Shoe and tire manufacturers maintain records of each pattern they produce for each model of shoe or tire. In the early 1990s, the body of a transvestite who hung around downtown bars was discovered in a narrow and out-of-the-way alley one morning. The victim was nearly nude, except for a bra and a pair of panties. Just beneath the bra and directly over the victim's heart, investigators found a partial print of the sole of a shoe. We could clearly see the letters R E E B and a partial pattern. We later learned that the victim was last seen in a bar with a group of men who claimed to have been from a navy ship at Pearl Harbor. The autopsy showed that blunt force trauma ruptured the victim's heart. The man was stomped to death. The implication was that the victim—convincingly dressed as a woman— met a group of men who thought he was a woman, and when they found out differently, they reacted violently.

We photographed the impression on a one-to-one (1:1) basis, which is actual size, and sent the photos to the Reebok factory on the mainland. The company responded that the pattern on the sole was found on a style manufactured and sold in San Diego. That fit with the information that the suspects might have been sailors. Unfortunately, we were not able to identify a suspect in that case. But in other cases, castings have helped provide critical evidence.

In another case, a Pearl City drug dealer was kidnapped one night by at least two men, according to friends who witnessed the kidnapping. We later learned that his abductors drove to an isolated spot off Renton Road in the 'Ewa Beach area. They backed their car into a narrow dirt lane, pulled the victim from the car, and took him to the front of the vehicle, where the headlights illuminated him. They shot him in the head, execution style, and his body fell straight to the ground in front of the car. The killers jumped back in the car and ran over his body in their vehicle as they fled the scene. When detectives examined his body the next day, they noticed two different tire patterns running across his legs. The victim was wearing shorts, so the tire prints were especially clear on his skin. The prints were photographed in great detail at the scene, while the victim lay in the dirt. Other tire prints were photographed, and castings were made in the dirt alongside his body. When investigators learned the identity of possible suspects, they went to a home in Waipahu to speak to one of the men. The detectives examined the tires of a vehicle in the driveway and noticed that the tread pattern bore a strong resemblance to those photographed and cast at the murder scene. When interviewing the suspect, the detectives confronted him with this information and he subsequently confessed to driving the car. He identified another man as the actual killer.

In the Rodrigues case, investigators were not successful in locating any impression evidence that would help us at that time identify her killer.

Knowing that we would not be able to complete the crime-scene investigation before sunset, we worked with the evidence specialists to set up large lights that would help us continue into the night. Even with the lights, the going was slow. We had to sift carefully through the garbage, trying not to miss anything that could provide evidence to the killer's identity.

That Pauline had been dead for several days was immediately apparent. In addition to the bloating and discoloration of her body, part of her scalp and hair had come free of her skull, and there were semicircle tears to the skin of her face around her mouth and nose.

She also had maggot infestation at several places on her body. We called for Dr. Lee Goff to come to the scene and conduct a study of the insect infestation to help determine time of death.

Dr. Goff was at the time a forensic entomologist at the University of Hawai'i and had assisted HPD with various investigations in which insect activity was present. Flies land on a body and lay eggs very shortly after someone dies. These eggs develop into maggots that subsequently develop into larvae and then into adult flies. Dr. Goff collects maggots, larvae, and adult flies and takes them back to his lab. There he examines the specimens and grows the maggots to adulthood. Using the specimens and case studies, he can then determine, rather accurately, the time of death.

Except for three rings on the woman's left hand, she was nude. Her body was taken to the morgue, and an autopsy was scheduled for Saturday morning. Worried that we would miss something in the dark, we had officers remain at the scene and protect it from contamination. We would return on Saturday to complete the crime-scene investigation.

By Saturday afternoon, we had finished the scene work and knew that the victim had died of asphyxiation. The pathologist told us that a portion of the victim's clothing was found jammed into her throat. In addition, she had those semicircle cuts around her mouth and nose.

Within a few days, we had come to believe that the body was that of Pauline Rodrigues. It was not possible to conduct fingerprint analysis because of the advanced decomposition of her body. We could not identify her through dental records because we could not locate dental x-rays to use for comparison. The clearest piece of evidence that the woman found murdered in Hau Bush was Pauline Rodrigues came from a high school photo of Pauline that our Missing Persons Detail had that showed her with three gold rings on her left hand. They were the same three rings found on the left hand of the woman in Hau Bush. In cases where there is not enough evidence to prove positive identification, circumstantial evidence can be accepted, as in this case. That presumptive identification helped put that young woman to rest.

Months passed with no leads as to the identity of Pauline's killer, and the case fell to inactive status. Sometime later, a woman who was suspected of being a drug dealer was found beaten and stabbed in her apartment, with a corkscrew twisted into one of her breasts. The indication was that this woman's death was a sexual murder. Detectives developed a suspect in that case named "Shorty."

By the time the detectives had enough information to warrant talking to Shorty, he was already in jail for another crime. Detectives met Shorty inside O'ahu Prison for an interview regarding the murder of the drug dealer. In no time, Shorty confessed to killing that woman. He then told the detectives that he wanted to talk to them about the murder of another woman. The detectives listened as Shorty described the abduction and murder of Pauline Rodrigues.

He described how he enticed her into his truck on Waimano Home Road, pretending to offer her a ride to Pearl City High School. Instead, he drove up to the end of the road to a construction site. There he raped her and decided to kill her. He tried to strangle her, but he told the detectives that she wouldn't die. He then took her skirt and jammed it into her mouth, pushing it down her throat. It wouldn't go all the way down, so he got a pipe and, standing over her, used the pipe to jam the cloth down her throat. After a little while she stopped moving. She appeared dead, so he pulled her up into the bed of his truck, covered her with some construction debris, and drove to Hau Bush, where he dumped her body into a garbage dump.

The detectives knew of the case he was describing, but it was a case that was assigned to other detectives, so they made arrangements with Shorty to have the other detectives come back the next day. Shorty agreed. But he had other plans. The next morning before the detectives arrived to interrogate him, Shorty took a handgun from a guard and broke out of prison. He hijacked a car and fled. Shorty was gone.

About two weeks after he escaped from prison, Pearl City officers got a tip that Shorty and others were holed up in a Waipahu housing complex. Two officers responded to the second-floor apartment where he allegedly was hiding. When the door opened, the officers were looking down the barrel of a gun, and one of the officers was taken hostage. Hostage negotiators and the highly trained SWAT (Specialized Weapons And Tactics) team were called, and soon the apartment complex was surrounded. Negotiations for the officer's release began, and surprisingly, the officer was released unharmed. But soon after the officer was allowed to go free, gunshots came from the apartment. Occasionally, more gunshots were fired, and SWAT found it impossible to get some of the residents to evacuate their homes, because some might come under gunfire if they left. Negotiations with the suspects went nowhere. Soon, the command decision was made. The HPD administration thought it was the only possible decision in order to protect the community from the random gunfire that was coming from the apartment. Take Shorty out.

The plan was set. The SWAT officers would fire tear gas into the apartment. Other officers, positioned near the apartment's front door, would burst in when the tear gas filled the room and attempt to arrest Shorty. They had authority to use deadly force if Shorty attempted to fire upon them. But those officers never got to put that plan into action. The tear gas fired into the apartment ignited a fire, which quickly spread.

The fire department was called, but because someone from inside the apartment was shooting at people outside, firefighters rightfully refused to respond until he was in custody. Within minutes, the shooting stopped, and a one-legged man came to a window, shouting for help. He jumped from the second-floor window and SWAT officers placed him under arrest. There was no sign of Shorty. Minutes later the apartment was engulfed in flames, and the fire department rolled up and put out the blaze under the protection of SWAT. Firefighters who entered the apartment to completely extinguish the blaze found Shorty's body in the bathroom, his rifle at his side.

The murder case of Pauline Rodrigues was closed based on

Shorty's confession. He knew facts about the murder that no one else knew—that no one else could have known except the killer.

One of the officers involved in the case said it best perhaps. Dying in the fire seemed only fitting for Shorty, after all the pain he inflicted on his victims.

It was like his personal invitation to hell.

10

The Disappearance of Jie-Zhao Li, Therese Rose Vanderheiden-Walsh, and Peter Boy Kema

On February 11, 1988, the unthinkable happened in Honolulu. A twelve-year-old girl was abducted off the street in a busy part of town in broad daylight. There have been other cases of child abduction in Hawai'i, but this was the first in which a child was abducted by a stranger, never to be found again. You read of such cases in news reports from mainland cities, but people say, "It doesn't happen here." But it has happened here.

Jie-Zhao Li was taken by a stranger. Not so in the case of Therese Rose Vanderheiden-Walsh. Francis Walsh was divorced from his wife, Merle Marie Vanderheiden, but was granted custody of his five-year-old daughter, Therese. Merle, who was known to disappear for periods of time, was, however, granted supervised visitation. On June 22, 1990, while Francis was at work and Therese was at a youth program at Kokokahi YWCA, Merle, violating the court order, went to the YWCA and abducted Therese, two weeks before her sixth birthday.

The FBI issued a warrant for Merle's arrest on August 2, 1990. The warrant has remained unserved. Merle had a reputation for using many disguises and aliases, and it's believed that she has been on the run with Therese since the abduction, using different names and living in different cities. As the years passed, the FBI periodically released drawings that showed what Therese might look like as she grew older. Therese's father, Francis, worked with the FBI and law enforcement in many states in his effort to find his abducted daughter—to no avail, and to his greatest sorrow. Francis Walsh died on September 7, 1998.

Like Jie-Zhao Li and Therese Vanderheiden-Walsh, "Peter Boy"

Kema, Jr., is a missing child. He was reported missing on September 11, 1997. His father claims to have left him in the custody of a woman named Auntie Rose Makuakane at ʻAʻala Park in Honolulu. The boy's maternal grandparents, James and Yolanda Acol, of Kona, had taken care of Peter Boy since he was three months old. He was taken from the custody of his parents because of suspected abuse resulting in a broken leg. The *Honolulu Star-Bulletin,* in an article dated May 1, 1999, reported that the state ordered the return of Peter Boy to his parents, and that the Acols last saw him in 1996. Ask people what they think happened to Peter Boy, and many will tell you they think he was a victim of foul play. Most believe he is dead. The police investigation was given to the prosecutors, but no arrests have been made in the case.

Many people believe that Jie-Zhao Li, like Peter Boy, met with foul play. Many police officers believe that she was murdered, especially those of us who worked on the case and investigated her disappearance. But there are some, especially those connected with missing children foundations, who believe that Jie-Zhao Li was abducted and is alive somewhere. They have to believe that. Because not every abducted child is murdered. And not every case shows evidence of a murder. And because they need to maintain a hope and a wish that this child has somehow survived. A hope and a wish that this child will one day be old enough and strong enough to walk away—to run away—from her captors. A hope and a wish that all the abducted children will run away and return to the families who love them and miss them.

Jie-Zhao was a twelve-year-old student who was spending the afternoon of February 11, 1988, selling Zippy's chili tickets for a fundraiser. She was going door to door in her neighborhood and walking along Nuʻuanu Avenue. She was last seen in the parking lot of the 7-11 store at the intersection of Nuʻuanu Avenue and Kuakini Street, just a few blocks from her home. She would approach people going into or coming out of the store, asking if they wanted to buy some chili. Witnesses reported that she was speaking to people in their cars and that she may have gotten into an old Chevy sedan. The car was described as a 1955, 1956, or 1957 Chevy.

We were on this case almost from the beginning. Detectives from the Missing Persons Unit and the Homicide Detail, along with all the uniformed officers that the Patrol Division could spare from their normal duties, canvassed the streets for about a mile from the 7-11 store where she was last seen. Officers wrote hundreds of follow-up reports detailing any piece of information any possible witness could offer. We looked up and down every street. We searched every residential backyard. We checked every storm drain. We walked the banks of every river and canal. There was no sign of Jie-Zhao Li.

At the start of the investigation, that old Chevy sedan became a critical piece of information, and we chased that lead as hard as we could. The staff at the Research and Development Division helped out by producing a computer printout of all the registered Chevys from the early 1950s, when the box-shaped model first came out, until the design change of the 1959 model. We thought there would be thirty to fifty registered cars that old. There were hundreds. A detective was assigned to go to each registered address, look at the car, speak to the owner, and question him or her in relation to this case. Although the witness could not be sure that Jie-Zhao actually got into the Chevy, we had to assume that she did, and investigate as if she did. Anything less would be unprofessional and incomplete.

We worked with the media to seek the public's assistance. We distributed flyers, issued news releases, and asked the public to provide us with any information they could. Many, many calls came in. "I saw that missing little girl in Wai'anae." "I saw her in Waialua." "That '55 Chevy you're looking for is parked at Sunset Beach, and there's a little Chinese girl inside. She was tied to the seat and she looked very afraid."

We followed all the leads. Not one call was left unanswered. And many a time, police officers sped through intersections and down roadways with sirens screaming and blue lights flashing to get to the location where Jie-Zhao was reportedly seen. But all of the leads were false. Then one day, a patrol officer gave us the name of a young man who the officer thought had problems with young girls. The officer told us that he had handled several minor cases in which this young man had harassed young girls on Nu'uanu Avenue. We became very interested.

We found the man simply by waiting at the intersection of Nu'uanu and Kuakini—the site of Jie-Zhao's abduction. He was friendly and cooperative, but something in his manner didn't seem quite right. There was something to his behavior that worried us. We soon learned that he was paranoid-schizophrenic. From the moment we stopped to speak to him, he talked to us. And each time we spoke to him, he opened up to us more and more. And then he began to speak to us in the third person, using the pronoun "he" during his discussions with us. We continued to speak to him on various occasions, and suddenly, this young man told us that "he took her up to Nu'uanu Stream." We organized a search team to hunt for evidence. The team walked the stream. Again, there was nothing. We tried to get this young man to open up more by asking, "Will he take us to her?" No luck. Many of us had a feeling that he was involved in Jie-Zhao's disappearance.

Then one day, after numerous attempts to get him to "show us where she is" failed, we simply told him not to come back. We weren't getting any further. Maybe acting like we didn't believe him anymore would push him to reveal something. We hoped the strategy would get him to cooperate more or bring us some evidence to prove to us that he had knowledge of her disappearance. Again, that led us nowhere. He did come back and make some threats against us. He actually showed up at my home armed with a gun while I was at an FBI homicide seminar in Quantico, Virginia. He was arrested and spent more time under psychiatric care. It was disturbing that he found my home, but it was probably because he had relatives who lived a few houses away and might have seen me there. In spite of all the attempts to interrogate him, no new evidence developed to prove that he was involved in Jie-Zhao's abduction.

The recent murder of eleven-year-old Kahealani Indreginal of 'Aiea differed from Jie-Zhao's in the relationship between killer and victim. Indreginal, who lived at the Pu'uwai Momi housing complex near Pearl Harbor, was observed by witnesses getting into the blue Dodge Neon owned by twenty-year-old Christopher Aki, the boyfriend of Indreginal's half-sister, Tanya Mamala-Tumbaga. That was on December 10, 2002. It was the last time she was seen alive. A hiker discovered her body on Friday, December 13, 2002, about seventy-two hours after she was seen near her home.

Police arrested Aki after he confessed to Kahealani's murder. A police source, described by *Honolulu Advertiser* reporters as being close to the investigation, said that Aki told investigators that he took her to the 'Aiea Loop Trail, at the top of 'Aiea Heights Drive. There, for reasons not explained, she slapped him and he beat her, both in and outside his car, with a metal pipe. He told police that he later threw the pipe into Hālawa Stream. Police divers did not find the murder weapon. Police spokesmen have said that they suspect drugs were involved in the killing.

Aki was charged with second-degree murder, and his bail was set at 5 million dollars. Prosecutor Peter Carlisle told reporters that he will seek enhanced sentencing for Aki, if he is convicted of Indreginal's murder. Second-degree murder carries a penalty of life in prison with the possibility of parole. Enhanced sentencing would mean that, if convicted, Aki would receive a sentence of life in prison without the possibility of parole.

Shortly before Indreginal's abduction and murder, the Honolulu Police Department announced the activation of the Maile alert. This program, like others across the United States, provides for a quick release of information about a child's abduction to the public. The hope is that someone in the community will hear the information, be on the alert, and report information to the police.

The Maile alert is named for 6-year-old Maile Gilbert, who was abducted from a party on Iliwahi Loop in Kailua in August of 1985. She was taken to Waialua, where she was murdered and buried in the sand at a beach park.

Do such alerts work? Yes! In California in 2002, two teenaged girls were abducted at gunpoint. An Amber alert, named after a girl who was abducted and murdered, was broadcast, giving information on the kidnapper's vehicle. Motorists saw the suspect's car in the California desert, many miles from the scene of the abduction. Responding police stopped the suspect's car, and in a shootout with the kidnapper, killed him. The girls reported that they were raped by the kidnapper, and police suspected that he was planning to murder them.

It can't be said too many times that if anyone has any information concerning the disappearance of Jie-Zhao Li, Therese Vanderheiden-Walsh, Peter Boy Kema, Jr., or any other missing child, call the police. Speak for the children who have no voice. Don't be afraid that the information you may be passing on is not true or accurate. That's not your worry. It's the job of every police officer in this country to follow up on information given to them on criminal cases, especially missing children. If they don't, they're not true to their vow to protect and serve the people in their community. If for some reason you don't want to contact the police, you may contact the Hawai'i State Clearinghouse on Missing Children at (808) 586-1449 or (808) 753-9797 or the National Center for Missing and Exploited Children at 1-800-843-5678.

In a *Star-Bulletin* article on January 12, 2002, reporter Suzanne Tswei wrote that Jie-Zhao's mother, Li Yan Li, finally received her U.S. citizenship, realizing a long-awaited dream. She said she is left with one wish yet to be fulfilled—that Jie-Zhao will one day come home.

11
The Rampage of John Miranda

John Nahale Miranda stood six feet five inches tall and weighed 260 pounds. Some called him a "gentle giant," while others feared him as a moody man with a bad attitude. Just before Christmas in 1995, Miranda was fired from his job at Seal Masters, a waterproofing company located on Sand Island, an industrial area not far from Honolulu International Airport. While most people simply walk away angry from jobs that don't work out, Miranda decided to get even. And about six weeks later—fueled by a deadly mix of cocaine, crystal methamphetamine, and marijuana—he walked into his former workplace with a sawed-off shotgun. He took five hostages, fired at his former coworkers, shooting one in the leg, and even called a popular morning radio show to talk about what he was doing. He kept police at bay, emerging from the building to show them that he had taped the shotgun to the neck of one worker and to his own right hand. Seven hours later, the tension skyrocketed as Miranda began what he described as a countdown to the death of his hostage and police shot him before that could happen. He died minutes later.

The incident took hours and was dramatically documented by photographers and reporters, who watched as the tension built. Much of the day's events unfolded on live television, adding to the public spectacle. When it was over, company vice-president Guy George had been shot, employee Tom McNeil had had a shotgun duct-taped to his neck for at least five hours, all the employees were terrorized, and Miranda was dead.

But the damage didn't end there. Two weeks after the standoff at Sand Island, another victim was found. Police had been searching for Miranda's girlfriend, Sherry Lynn Holmes, who disappeared before

Miranda took the hostages. They found the body of the thirty-two-year-old Holmes, a bar hostess, buried in a shallow grave along Kawainui Marsh in Kailua. She had been strangled. Among the evidence linking Miranda to her murder were his own statements to people about "burying somebody" and a history of domestic violence.

$$\oplus$$

On February 6, 1996, Seal Masters opened up at 6:30 A.M. as on any other work day. Less than half an hour later, Miranda walked into the building with a sawed-off, 12-gauge shotgun and ordered everyone there to lie on the floor. Those workers remember him saying: "Hi guys, remember me? This is no joke."

As other workers arrived, he told them to sit down, and by 7:45 A.M., someone had called 911. About fifteen minutes later, Miranda moved George into a smaller office and fired twice, breaking the office window and shattering the door. Then he shot George in the right leg. Around 9 A.M., Miranda went to the bathroom, giving George a chance to lock himself in the office. Twenty-five minutes later he dragged himself to a window, climbed out, and fell to the ground, leaving a trail of blood on the wall as he escaped. An ambulance rushed him to The Queen's Medical Center in critical condition.

The twenty-eight-year-old disgruntled ex-worker blamed others for his inability to keep a job. He said that they were fueled by racism directed at him because he was part-Hawaiian and Puerto Rican. He predicted from the start that someone was going to die, and it was clear from his early conversations that day that he believed he would be among those who would die. This left police in an especially sensitive situation as they tried to negotiate a peaceful end to the chilling drama.

While George was escaping, Miranda was calling the KSSK morning radio show to complain that mainland bosses mistreat local workers. Hosts Larry Price and Michael W. Perry taped the conversation, then aired it later. Some of the exchange hints at how troubled and angry Miranda appeared that day. But the conversation also hints at his contradictions: desperate and wounded, paranoid and violent, but a proud parent.

KSSK: What happened to cause you to do all this?

Miranda: I don't know, I guess just stress . . . , you know.

KSSK: Now, you're not going to do anything . . . weird here, right?

Miranda: Well, believe me, those people going die. I sure ain't going to prison.

KSSK: No, you're not. Calm down now.

Miranda: Well, buddy, bruddah [George] already missing part of his leg, so I ain't joking.

KSSK: Hey, that's not. You know, we can help you out here.

Miranda: Oh, too late.

KSSK: How many years you work there?

Miranda: About four years.

KSSK: What do you do there?

Miranda: Waterproofing. But you know this just sucks, man. I was good, good, but apparently this guy didn't care, he just use us local boys. Treat us like trash. And the mainland boys come down or white boys, whatever, you know, they just get favoritism. You know, I mean they get everything on a silver platter when they work for this company. So, it's kinda you could say this man is a racist and I'm the . . . black Hawaiian KKK . . . Nah, I'm just kidding.

KSSK: Oh, you don't have to go that far.

Miranda: Well, bruddah, it's too late now.

KSSK: You got family?

Miranda: Yeah, I got a beautiful daughter. Man, I'm gonna miss her.

KSSK: No, you're not gonna miss her. You're not gonna leave her now.

Miranda: I have a beautiful girl. Man, she is everything to me.

KSSK: Why would you leave? What's her name?

Miranda: I feel I lost it . . . lost it.

He called two radio stations and *The Honolulu Advertiser* that day and his demeanor changed from victimized to defiant. Shortly after George escaped through the window, Miranda and three hostages emerged on an outdoor stairway. Once they came out of the building, the incident became a public spectacle, with the police, news crews, and growing crowd of spectators all watching Miranda's every move. Miranda blamed George for his latest problems, saying he never told him when he could go back to work. When Miranda walked the three out of the building, two of the men ran away—one released by Miranda, the other fleeing when he had the chance—leaving McNeil with the shotgun taped to his neck. With live television tracking the situation, workers across the state kept an eye on the situation.

The two men paced back and forth. They went up and down the steps. Sometimes, Miranda sat down. He even flashed a smile, while McNeil stared downward. Police provided a cellular phone to Miranda. He stopped to get drinks and smoke cigarettes while everyone continued waiting and watching and waiting.

At one point, Miranda told negotiators to give him twenty thousand dollars. Police responded to the demand, showing him packs of one hundred dollar bills and promising they would be his if he released McNeil. At that point, Miranda shifted gears again and told police to take the money to the gas station on a nearby corner and throw it into the air.

McNeil's girlfriend watched in horror as his life dangled at the end of a shotgun taped to an erratic and violent man.

People began to describe Miranda to the police and reporters. He was a former high school varsity football player at Castle High School in Kāne'ohe, where he graduated in 1985. Other friends recalled how he'd avoid body contact while playing basketball with friends. Some talked about his darker side. Court records indicated he'd been arrested on suspicion of first-degree burglary after forcing his way into an apartment and threatening to throw his neighbor off the lanai. Miranda admitted to yelling and talking loud, but denied any threats and was convicted of a lesser misdemeanor charge.

Six years before the standoff, he was arrested for abusing a woman and ordered to substance abuse treatment and counseling, but he didn't go to treatment. An acquaintance who coached Miranda in an adult touch-tackle football league saw a moody man who got picked for the team because of his size, not his attitude. But others saw a big man tenderly in love with his two-year-old daughter, Tehani, even though his relationship with her mother had faded.

While Miranda's background became clearer, members of the highly trained Specialized Services Division were poised outside as Miranda continued the standoff. Police waited in force, with sharp-shooters on the roof and a dozen men clad in body armor and shields moving closer to the standoff. Just before 11 A.M. Miranda untaped the shotgun from his right hand, took off his jacket, and taped the shotgun to his left hand. Another fifteen minutes went by and Miranda and McNeil walked down the stairs to the edge of Sand Island Access Road. After armed police surrounded him, Miranda backed away and forced McNeil to go back up the stairs.

At 1:24 that afternoon, Miranda again forced McNeil to walk downstairs and to the edge of the road and then headed back toward the building. Just before 2:30 P.M., Miranda announced his plan to count down and then kill McNeil. He started counting at sixty and got to fifteen before hostage McNeil tried to twist away. Police fired and Miranda fell. McNeil walked to an ambulance and then was taken to St. Francis Medical Center, where he was treated for scrapes and bruises.

By the time police shot him, Miranda's relatives had joined the growing audience. An older brother, Donald Rodrigues, had to be tackled by police when he ran toward Miranda as the shots tore through him, shouting, "That's my brother! That's my brother!"

A half-dozen officers stopped the angry and frustrated Rodrigues as he cursed and kicked and asked what family and friends often do at these volatile scenes. "Why didn't you let us help? Why? Why?"

Judging from my years of experience in charge of HPD's hostage negotiating team, I believe the officers at the scene followed the accepted standard in handling the Miranda standoff. The police followed methods that have been honed by years of experience with similar situations. They refused to allow any of Miranda's relatives to speak directly to him, in person or on the phone. But they did allow a sister to tape-record a message to him.

People have criticized the police, not only in this case, but in other hostage incidents, for not allowing family to intervene. Some have said that the police are not sensitive to the Hawaiian custom of *ho'oponopono*, a cultural method of working out problems.

But police aren't being mean or insensitive; they are striving to protect as many people as possible in a hostage situation. It is an established fact that family of hostage takers have made situations worse. And one major consideration is that many hostage takers are merely trying to commit "suicide by cop," and when allowed to speak to family, use the incident to say goodbye. Hostages have been killed, forcing the police to use deadly force against the hostage taker— exactly what Miranda seemed to want.

Negotiators work very hard to establish a calm rapport with a suspect, to keep the lines of communication open, and to prevent a violent end. Those goals usually rule out allowing distraught relatives to jump in and further crank up the emotion and the dangers to all involved. It's easy to understand how frustrating that can be for the family, but the policy emerged only after negotiators over time did allow emotionally involved relatives to escalate such situations.

And that explains why you see police wait for hours; you see landline telephones delivered while the regular telephone lines are cut, preventing the hostage taker from making calls; you see cold drinks and hot food passed to barricaded suspects, but you're unlikely to see police hand a bull-horn or a telephone to a family member. In most cases, it simply doesn't help. In some cases, it can be a fatal mistake.

Then-Police Chief Michael Nakamura, a kind and calm man, was clearly personally saddened by the violent end to the Miranda standoff. Nevertheless, he stood strongly behind the police decision to shoot Miranda rather than risk the death of McNeil.

"He counted from sixty and at the time he got to fifteen, the hostage made a decision to try and escape," Nakamura said. When McNeil pulled his head away from the shotgun's muzzle, police had a split-second opportunity to intervene.

"If the sharpshooters didn't take action at that time that hostage would have also been dead," Nakamura said.

Miranda's former boss, Dick Spies, shook his head when the day was over. He said Miranda was an excellent worker "when his head was on straight" but a troublemaker when it was not.

After it was all over, the former hostage, McNeil, called radio station KRTR-FM to urge people to enjoy life. "Everybody out there listening, go home tonight and hug your wife or hug your kids. Because you just never know, you just never know what's going to happen."

In another conversation with the radio station, McNeil told listeners he was fine but sorry that Miranda had to die. He wasn't critical of police, and he discounted Miranda's claims of racism. McNeil said that he pleaded with Miranda throughout the day to drop the gun and choose life, but he said Miranda kept talking about not wanting to go back to jail. Miranda seemed determined to die.

In hostage cases that go on for long periods of time, a condition develops called the Stockholm Syndrome. The hostages, who are so dependent on the hostage taker for their survival, actually develop empathy for the suspect. This usually begins after many hours of being a hostage. The hostage taker allows a small kindness, such as food or permission to go to the bathroom. It's a sign that the suspect is human and perhaps will not hurt them after all. With more time, the hostages begin to feel that the police are the reason they are still hostages. If the cops would simply go away, they would be safe. In some cases, the hostages even defend the motives of the hostage taker.

This didn't occur in the Miranda case. McNeil knew that his life was in extreme danger from Miranda's irrational acts. Miranda acted as if life meant nothing to him during those moments. Having apparently strangled his girlfriend, Sherry Holmes, and shot Guy George, he seemingly thought there was no further reason for him to live. Not even his daughter.

And the rampage of John Miranda came to an end on Sand Island Access Road.

12
The Mass Murder at the Xerox Corporation

The worst mass murder in the state of Hawai'i's recorded history took place on an unremarkable day that started out like many weekdays everywhere and ended with the deaths of seven good men. It was November 2, 1999, a Tuesday.

The men were killed by a coworker, someone whom many of them had wondered and worried about before—because of his odd work habits, an angry episode earlier at their workplace, and a general sense that he was trouble.

All the men were at work on the second floor of the Xerox Engineering Systems Building in an industrial area along Nimitz Highway, not far from Honolulu International Airport. They were gathered for an 8 A.M. employee team meeting. Five minutes after that meeting was to begin, employees in the warehouse heard shots fired. Some employees of nearby businesses then saw a man leave the building quickly and quietly, jumping into a green Ford Aerostar van emblazoned with the Xerox company name.

A city emergency medical team responded just two minutes later after calling for an assist from the Honolulu Fire Department, but they arrived to find seven victims dead and no one injured. Other medical and fire units were turned away, leaving police to sort out the crime.

That day, seven families lost members they counted on and would never see again. And they were gone in minutes. People listening to their radios heard another report of workplace violence. Then they realized in horror that this wasn't some news report from far away—that it had happened here, and all they could do now was learn more about those who were dead and wait for the police to piece together the trail, find the killer, and bring him to trial.

The victims were

Jason Balatico, thirty-three, of Kalihi Valley, the youngest of the men who died. He was a copier repairman up for promotion who left behind his wife, Merry Lynn, and their young son and daughter.

Ford Kanehira, forty-one, a copier technician who lived in Kāne'ohe with his wife, Lorna, and their five-year-old son. Coworkers described him as a friendly member of "the lunch bunch." His wife describes a best friend, a devoted husband and father, and the love of her life.

Ron Kataoka, fifty, of Mililani, who grew up in Wahiawā, graduated from Leilehua High School in 1966, attended Honolulu Community College, and served in the military in Vietnam.

Ron Kawamae, fifty-four, who lived in Makiki and was remembered as a karaoke singer who had suffered the death of his seventy-five-year-old father. He had worked for Xerox for more than thirty years as a copier technician who held some supervisory duties and helped train new employees. He is survived by a son and a grandson.

Peter Mark, forty-six, of Hawai'i Kai, a copier repairman who had worked for Xerox since 1981. He was a cousin of fellow shooting victim Melvin Lee. Mark was described as someone who loved the outdoors. He left behind his wife, Karen, and two children.

Melvin Lee, fifty-eight, a field service manager for Xerox who lived in Waipi'o Gentry, and who was looking forward to retirement in two years after thirty-two years in the workforce. He was planning to spend more time with family and work on his golf game. Lee was born and raised in 'Aiea, served on his neighborhood board, and worked on a community policing project. He is survived by his wife, Ann, two sons, and a daughter.

John Sakamoto, thirty-six, a fisherman who grew up in Hawai'i Kai and kept his boat at his parents' house. He was a copier repairman, survived by his wife, Susan, a daughter, and a son.

Police arrived at the scene just before the ambulance and found the seven dead men. Employees reeling from the enormity of the tragedy identified the coworker-turned-killer: Byran K. Uyesugi.

News seeped out slowly on radio and TV, as employees of nearby businesses said they heard shots, the ambulance arrived, and reports of injuries, then deaths, emerged. Police issued an all-points-bulletin for the forty-year-old copier repairman.

Eventually a portrait emerged of Uyesugi, a man who lived with his father and brother in an old neighborhood in Nu'uanu on a road with an unlikely name: Easy Street. Uyesugi raised koi, or Japanese carp, in huge tanks in his backyard, built furniture, collected guns, and mostly kept to himself.

It was clear that Uyesugi's preoccupation with guns began early. Uyesugi attended Roosevelt High School, a public school that serves much of urban Honolulu, graduating in 1977. By his junior year, he was on the riflery team, and the school's 1975 yearbook shows him lying on the ground, peering over a rifle. The caption reads: "Utilizing the spotting scope, resolute rifleman Byran Uyesugi focuses on the target."

Prior to becoming the most infamous murderer in recent Hawai'i history, Uyesugi had little contact with police. His criminal record turned up a drunk driving conviction from 1985, a misdemeanor. And police noted only one other incident: in 1993 he was arrested on suspicion of third-degree criminal property damage after he kicked an elevator door at Xerox after arguing with coworkers. That case was dismissed a year later.

Within an hour of the killings, police had evacuated a downtown office building that housed other Xerox employees and had gone to the Nu'uanu home Uyesugi shared with his widowed father and brother. Then-Governor Ben Cayetano ordered public access to the state capitol to be limited after the shootings, and word quickly spread that Uyesugi was a frequent visitor to the capitol, where several powerful copy machines crank out the reams of bills and reports of the state legislature.

By that afternoon, his stunned father, Hiroyuki Uyesugi, turned over eighteen weapons owned by Byran, including eleven handguns, five rifles, and two shotguns.

While the frantic search for the gunman continued, fellow workers and family members sorted out who was dead. Uyesugi had headed to Makiki, but the shock of the news frayed people's nerves, and police had reports that he had turned up in Kaimukī, Nuʻuanu and finally Makiki. By 9:45 A.M., a woman jogging spotted him sitting in the Xerox van near the Hawaiʻi Nature Center, in a scenic wooded area just minutes from downtown Honolulu.

The nature preserve is popular, and that day was no exception, with two elementary schools visiting that morning, one group already on the trail, the other ordered to keep the field trip inside the center until any danger subsided.

Police—including officers from the highly trained Specialized Weapons and Tactics team, better known as SWAT, which includes snipers trained to kill when needed—quickly and quietly swarmed the area. Uyesugi's brother, Dennis, a state worker, headed toward the Makiki Heights area to help police in negotiations with the armed killer.

Police negotiation specialists also arrived and arranged to get Uyesugi a cellular phone so that they could talk. Police said they believed that Uyesugi considered shooting himself, but most of the time seemed intent on giving himself up.

By eleven that morning, family members of the employees began to arrive at the shooting scene. Many had heard reports of shots fired and then tried to page or call their loved ones. About three hours later, police announced that they had notified family members of all the dead men.

At 2:51 P.M., Uyesugi got out of the company van in Makiki Heights, walked backward toward the back of the vehicle with his hands up, and then went to the ground. Police arrested him after the five-hour standoff and found one 9 mm gun in the van. By 3:30 P.M., Uyesugi was taken from the urban rain forest to police headquarters.

Detectives worked to piece together the events of the morning and to mull over a motive for the man who had shot five men in a conference room and two others in the office they shared.

The community shook with disbelief and with grief. Over and over, people wondered how such an awful crime could occur in Hawai'i, in the morning, at work, without some immediately obvious explosion.

Police and prosecutors pieced together the events this way: Uyesugi walked into work that morning with a Glock 9-mm semiautomatic pistol with a seventeen-round magazine hidden in a holster under his aloha shirt. He saw one coworker, but kept walking down the hall. Then he pulled out the gun and shot Ronald Kawamae in the back of the head, killing him instantly. Jason Balatico responded by running toward the gunman, who turned on him, shooting him in the wrist, chest, shoulder, neck, and back. He did not shoot another man who was in the room. Then Uyesugi continued down the hall, entered another room, assumed a "combat stance," and shot Melvin W. T. Lee, John Sakamoto, Ronald Kataoka, and Peter Mark. Uyesugi reloaded the pistol and shot Ford Kanehira five times. Most of the men were shot in the chest and back. Two of the men that Uyesugi passed by without shooting ran down the hall. Another coworker also headed out, as Uyesugi fired at least twice more at him before leaving the building by the back staircase.

With seven middle-class men dead, the connections were many: neighbors, family, school friends, classmates. While the first shock left many immediate family members wanting to be left alone, it took no time for others who knew the men to come forward.

On the day his younger son sat surrounded by police and wanted for the worst mass murder in the state's history, Hiroyuki Uyesugi quietly talked to reporters. Clearly shocked and ashamed by the brutal crime, the retired postal worker told them: "I am gonna bring him another gun so he can shoot himself. I would tell him to shoot himself."

The elder Uyesugi said that he and his son didn't talk about work when they were at home. But the father did say that the earlier work incident in which Byran kicked the elevator had cost him fifteen hundred dollars and sent Byran to two weeks of counseling for anger management.

Acquaintances expressed shock at the violent outburst of a man they saw as mild-mannered, reserved, without emotion. At Roosevelt High School and at the capitol, some workers described Uyesugi as patient, calm, and helpful, while others found him odd. Some described his sitting silently for hours in an office after he had completed his repairs.

During his trial came reports that he suffered from delusions and heard voices and believed a "black shadow" haunted him and caused problems for him.

On June 13, 2000, Uyesugi was convicted of first-degree murder by a state circuit court jury. The jury took about eighty minutes to reject Uyesugi's defense that he was insane at the time of the killings.

In August 2000, Circuit Judge Marie Milks listened to another hour of tearful, angry, and grief-stricken testimony from the families of the victims, who spelled out why Uyesugi should remain behind bars. Then Milks sentenced him to life in prison without parole, the state's harshest sentence and one that is mandatory for first-degree murder. She also ordered him to pay seventy thousand dollars in restitution, the amount given to families from the Crime Victim Compensation Fund, and $500 to the Balatico family for psychological treatment and prescription medication.

After Uyesugi's sentence, the news media received copies of previously confidential reports of mental health experts who evaluated Uyesugi. While the reports shed little insight into the crime, they did provide additional information about the killer. Uyesugi told the analysts that he was the target of a conspiracy and believed "bugs" or listening devices had been planted at his home.

But he also told the experts that his anger sprang from a pattern of harassment from coworkers, whom he believed were sabotaging him. When he described the killings, he did so "methodically and calmly" and even "smiled a few times" as he talked about the shootings.

Uyesugi continues to serve his prison sentence. Relatives of the victims filed a lawsuit against the Xerox Corporation and three of its executives, alleging that the three knew or should have known that

Uyesugi displayed violent tendencies as far back as six years before the shooting. A state judge rejected the claim, but there is still time for an appeal.

The lawsuit also indicated that the executives knew that Uyesugi had talked several times about killing his coworkers. The lawsuit cited the October 1993 confrontation, in which Uyesugi threatened to kill a coworker, as well as his admission to a psychiatric ward at Castle Medical Center that year and the criminal property damage arrest and counseling that followed.

Xerox moved out of the building where the shootings occurred.

Uyesugi defense attorney Jerel Fonseca told reporters that he believed his client got a fair trial. "The jury heard all of the facts and they made their decision based on the facts."

When the time came for the state parole board to make its decision on how long Uyesugi will serve, city prosecutor Peter Carlisle asked for a sentence based on the numbers of years that the seven victims might have been expected to live if they had not been gunned down that morning.

The Hawai'i Paroling Authority determined that Uyesugi should serve 235 years before being released. Xerox Corporation reportedly paid the families the equivalent of what the men would have earned if they had not been killed. But that didn't bring them back.

In addition to the seven murdered men, Uyesugi hurt so many: the wives, children, brothers, sisters, mothers, and friends who lost their loved ones permanently and without warning. Some family members remained angry throughout the trial, especially infuriated that the killer never said he was sorry for what he had done. Ron Kawamae's adult son, Reid, said he hopes Uyesugi suffers and is tortured by his delusions of a black shadow. "I'm glad that Hawai'i doesn't have the death penalty because I think suffering in jail would be much harder for him," said Reid Kawamae. "I hope that black shadow talks to him every night when he's sleeping. When he's just about ready to fall asleep, that black shadow wakes him up so he cannot sleep, like I cannot sleep."

Lorna Kanehira is one of the widows. She is still a busy mom, but did not go back to work until a little more than three years after the shootings. She found the downtown area where she had worked too painful and full of memories of the life her family once shared. She is pretty, poised, and proud of their son, now midway through elementary school. But she misses her husband.

She poured out some of her grief in a ten-page victim impact statement prepared for the trial. In the statement, she detailed the special relationship that she and her husband, Ford, or "Fordie," had after nearly twenty-five years together. She talked about the missed milestones in their son's life. He was only in kindergarten when his dad was taken from him. Since then, he's lost his first tooth, been in May Day programs, and excelled in school and sports.

Lorna remembers many special times together. She said her friends described theirs as the perfect marriage, close and happy. Nine months after his death, she said, "My friends have remarked that for as long as they've known me, it has always been 'Ford and Lorna.' I don't know how to be Lorna without Ford."

When she spoke to the court, she said, "I don't want anyone to feel sorry for us; I just want Fordie back. I feel his absence when I try to play baseball or basketball with my son and see his frustration because I just can't do it the way Dad did."

Lorna told the court that there is not one part of the lives of the families that was NOT impacted by the killings. "We cannot escape it. This has touched everyone I meet . . . someone always knows someone that is somehow connected—and everyone can tell you where he or she was that terrible morning."

Lorna painted a picture of a full and happy life wrapped around a close relationship that centered their lives. "We were inseparable. We would go everywhere together," she said. "Since I worked for the state government, my friends could never understand why I would use all of my vacation year after year. For me, it meant more to spend time with Ford than to save up those prized ninety days."

They were preparing for a stay-at-home vacation in November of

1999. "We had planned to go to the movies and to go biking together. Instead, I held his funeral services on the evening before our vacation was to begin."

Their son was sick and home from school that week. Lorna had stayed home one day, and Ford was going to stay with him the next, but he couldn't because he and Uyesugi and the other repairmen were all scheduled to be at a team meeting.

Lorna thinks back on Ford's hobbies—a saltwater aquarium, home projects, and fishing—and how he had shared them with their son. She said they had tried for more than ten years to have a child and were thrilled to have their son turn their twosome into a tight-knit trio.

Tall, slim, and pretty, Lorna has a smile that lights up her face, usually when she's talking about their son. She's kind, friendly, and funny but there are times when a distant look crosses her face. Sometimes, she is actually talking about Ford, sometimes she's just thinking about their life then and now. She and her son now live in a different neighborhood. Her living room is dominated by family photos, many of Ford, some of their whole family, and some of family and friends taken since Ford died. They depict a happy life and show how much Ford Kanehira remains a presence in their lives. Lorna still refers to him as her husband in a loving way that might lead a casual listener to think she was talking about someone who had just stepped out of the room or had another commitment that forced him to miss the gathering.

And Lorna clearly strives to do her best with their son, supportive of his activities, ready with the video camera at special events, beaming with parental pride. But there are still those moments when the loss rises up sharply: when a friend's trip to Disneyland reminds them of their own broken plans to visit there just a few months after that awful November day; when their son's breezy school computer description of life through an eight-year-old's eyes includes the information "My dad is in heaven."

The survivors keep alive their happier memories as they build their lives in a way they hadn't planned with a sadness about what could have been and what should have been. "Ford Kanehira was a very special man. He was my husband, my best friend, the father of my son, my lover, my protector, my security—he made me laugh and he made life worth living," recalls Lorna Kanehira. "There was so much joy in the simple life that we shared together. I know that in my lifetime no one will ever love me the way he did."

13

The Assassination of Troy Barboza

Police Officer Troy Barboza was probably awake when he was shot in the early morning hours of October 22, 1987, by California drug dealer Tony Williams. My frustration began that day when I was notified of the slaying. A fellow police officer lay dead in his home, gunned down. I needed to get there quickly. But I couldn't because I wasn't told of the murder until dawn and I was living in Mililani at the time. To get to the Mānoa Valley crime scene, I had to endure the early morning gridlock traffic, and even a blue light and a siren couldn't make that go away or move any faster.

More frustrating than the traffic was the fact that I appeared to be the last police official in the department notified about Barboza's murder. As the homicide lieutenant, I was responsible for the investigation, but it seemed that most of Honolulu got word of the murder before I got the urgent page. Quite some time after rushing from my house, I arrived at Barboza's home, the scene of the murder. A large number of cars were parked on the roadway leading to Barboza's small apartment. Patrol cars, cars of police administrators, and the cars and vans of the media all blocked the roadway.

Mistake number one: We set up the yellow crime-scene barrier tape along the curb, parallel to the house where Barboza's apartment was located. This allowed the media to come right up to the public side of the crime-scene barrier tape, far too close to allow police investigators to work without in-their-face questioning by reporters during the initial phase of the probe. We should have simply blocked the roadway to allow only neighborhood residents and police to enter or exit.

A crime scene has the potential to be the single most important part of the criminal investigation. It's from a crime scene that we link a suspect to the crime or to the victim. It is the location, including the avenues of approach or escape, where the suspect committed the offense. Too often we forget that there may have been some activity by the suspect outside the crime scene proper. Indoor crime scenes are identified by their clear and obvious boundaries such as walls, rooms, etc. Outdoor crime scenes are more difficult to establish because their boundaries are not immediately obvious. In both cases, responding officers should extend the boundaries of a crime scene beyond what may actually be necessary. The boundaries can easily be brought in later in the investigation.

We also learned that day that reporters and news photographers will do whatever it takes to do *their* job well. This included climbing onto the roof of an adjacent house and up into a mango tree in the lot to the rear of the crime scene in order to get more information and better photos and video.

In the 1980s the Honolulu Police Department needed to improve its media relations. (Most police departments need to improve their media relations. Just ask most reporters.) Our posture at that time was to provide the media with as little information as possible: only what kind of case it was, when it occurred, and very little else. In too many instances, other than giving this general, limited information, our standard response was "no comment." In nearly every case, this was not enough for the media. When Michael Nakamura became chief of police in the summer of 1990, he thought it was important to include the homicide lieutenant in a series of media-relations training sessions, with the instructions to be as open with the media as allowed by the constraints of policy or investigation. Chief Nakamura realized that the media play a big role in disseminating information to the public and that HPD could play a better part in that process. We needed to develop a more trusting relationship with the media, one that permitted mutual respect and understanding. Historically, police across the nation have considered the media their enemy, and the media have considered the police too close-mouthed about issues that the public "has the right to know."

Actually, nowhere in our Constitution, our Bill of Rights, or other governmental rules, regulations, or laws is there specifically spelled out a "public's right to know" the goings-on of criminal investigations. The police have the responsibility to withhold information that could damage or hinder criminal investigations. The community's interest in knowing details of a crime must be balanced with the police's need to withhold information about evidence known only to the police and to the person who committed that crime—as demonstrated in the Roland Kotani and Grace Imura-Kotani murder and suicide cases.

But on the day Troy Barboza was murdered, Nakamura wasn't yet chief, and those more media-savvy policies weren't ready for prime time. We were faced with reporters and photographers who demanded information that they could print or report on the radio or TV. It must have been painfully frustrating for them to hear time and again, "We cannot comment at this time." Sometime during the day, the chief held a press conference giving what little information we had to the media—information they already had from their own investigations.

Some officers, for various reasons, give unauthorized information to reporters. Perhaps these "anonymous police officials" who provide information, true or otherwise, to reporters wish to show them just how much they are in-the-know. Perhaps they get a feeling of power. Perhaps they want to get back at the police administration for some perceived injustice. Perhaps they don't see any harm in providing information to reporters. Whatever the reason, these anonymous police officials create more havoc for investigators than good. Their information, or misinformation, adds to the frenzy of data gathering and causes a strain in the police-media relationship. In Barboza's case, that relationship was strained from the beginning, as our reluctance to provide information about his murder grew.

Mistake number two: Police administrators and other officers not associated with the investigation entered and contaminated the crime scene. This mistake is common to police agencies across the nation. At several homicide seminars I've heard detectives and homicide commanders say that their administrators were all over this or that crime scene—touching this and that and contaminating wherever they went. The contamination is not deliberately intended to destroy evidence or impede the investigation. Police officers are inherently curious, and a really good cop is very curious by nature. But an experienced or smart investigator understands crime-scene preservation and tempers investigative curiosity to limit natural contamination.

When I arrived at the Barboza murder scene, I was disturbed to find a large number of officers of varying high rank milling about the patio adjacent to Barboza's apartment. The killer shot through the living-room window while standing on a small wall in that same

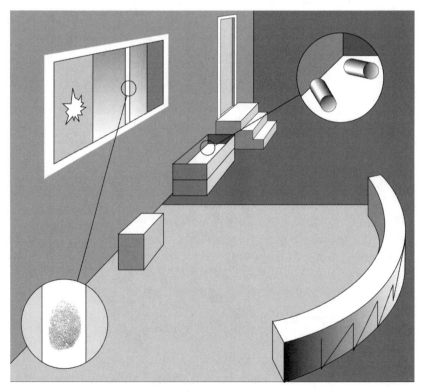

The patio where Tony Williams shot at Troy Barboza

patio. The patio was then, by definition, a part of the primary crime scene.

In their quest to understand what happened, many ranking officers entered Barboza's apartment, walked through it, and stood near his body. The walking around the apartment was in itself a problem. Barboza was killed by a blast from a shotgun. The fatal wound to his head filled the air in the living room with a fine mist of blood. The mist of blood settled on everything, including the floor. When the officers entered, they tracked this blood around the house. The tracks became visible when we conducted Luminol testing later.

Some contamination of a crime scene is expected. The first officers to respond must enter the room, emergency medical technicians must enter, and perhaps firefighters and other emergency personnel. But the standard investigative process is that when a person is pronounced dead, as was Barboza, everyone exits the scene and it is preserved as best as it can be after that. In the Barboza case, this rule was forgotten by some of the ranking officers. Perhaps they did not understand that simply walking through a crime scene, without touching anything, still contaminates it.

The first arriving officer or group of officers must be aware of myriad things prior to the arrival of the crime-scene investigators. They have a critically important task: to observe and document the scene at the time of their arrival, because that's probably what it looked like when the suspect left. In documenting the crime scene, officers look for answers to questions like these:

• Were the doors and windows found open or closed? Were they locked or unlocked?

• Were the lights on or off?

• Did the crime scene have a particular smell? Cigarettes, coffee, gasoline, perfume, food?

• Were there any signs of activities such as meal preparation or was half-eaten food on the table?

• Was there any indication of the date or time the crime was committed, such as newspapers collecting at the doorstep?

Initial officers at murder scenes need to find safe pathways through the crime scene—the routes that disturb as little evidence as possible. The officers must ensure that all who follow them stick to the safe pathways.

While the initial officers await the arrival of the crime-scene investigators, they can do multiple things while continuing to protect that crime scene: first, get the names of and other pertinent information from people who may be witnesses; keep witnesses from talking to each other about what they saw, to prevent them from influencing one another; establish the basic facts and document them, to provide as much information to the investigating team as possible; and listen quietly to the conversation of others, since important information can sometimes be learned simply by listening.

It is understandable that ranking police officials want to respond to the murder of one of their own officers. Out of a sense of responsibility and concern, they go to that crime scene and learn as much as they can. They reach out, they share grief, they show care, and they bear the burden of looking upon the body of that young officer, even praying over him. But no matter how noble the reason, these ranking officials must keep in mind that their presence is causing contamination, regardless of how careful they may feel they are. In Barboza's case, however, an issue of contamination arose that created a greater than usual concern.

Barboza's killer stood on a small concrete tile wall that abutted the living room's exterior wall. Because of the height of the windows, the killer couldn't stand on the ground and aim and shoot the weapon accurately. Two windows leading into the living room were separated by a thin strip of wood. On this strip of wood was a fingerprint. It was an extraordinarily fresh fingerprint. In the right light, you could see the ridge detail of the print that was left on the surface of the wood. Because this print was located next to the window through which the killer fired his weapon at Barboza, and because it was so fresh, it became an extremely important piece of evidence for us. Here, quite probably, was the killer's fingerprint. All we had to do was find the killer's name and do a comparison and we could have evidence that would help convict. We were extra careful. The surface of the wood was not perfectly smooth. It was a little wavy and pebbly because of the wood texture and paint. We were afraid that if we tried to dust and lift it with fingerprint lifting tape, we might not get the full print, which we could see clearly before us. So we dusted the print, photographed it, and covered it with fingerprint tape to help preserve it. We then recovered the wood that the print was on. An evidence specialist sawed away the thin strip of wood and preserved the latent print on the surface it was initially laid down upon. We would not risk damaging the print by trying to lift it.

Fingerprints are one of the most important items of evidence that investigators search for at crime scenes. Fingerprints remain unchanged during a person's life, unless altered deliberately or accidentally through scarring. They have individual characteristics. No two fingerprints have ever been found to be identical. Even identical twins have unique fingerprints.

Three types of fingerprint evidence can be left at crime scenes. "Plastic" fingerprints occur when fingers press against a moldable material, like putty. A negative impression is made of the finger's friction ridge pattern. Fingerprints "contaminated with a foreign matter" occur when fingers come into contact with blood, paint, or some similar substance and then touch an object, leaving the print behind. "Latent" fingerprints occur when fingers contaminated with perspiration and body acids and oils touch a surface and leave a print. Latents are the most common fingerprint evidence recovered from crime scenes. Depending on the environmental conditions, fingerprints can remain on a surface indefinitely.

The method used for recovery of fingerprints depends on the surface on which they are set down. Fingerprints on smooth surfaces are dusted with powder and then lifted with lifting tape, a tape specially prepared for this task; it does not have as much glue as commercial tape. The tape is then laid down on a clean white card and preserved on file. Other prints can be photographed or simply recovered with the object the print was on, as we did in Barboza's murder. Prints on human skin can be lifted the same way that prints on smooth surfaces are. They can also be lifted from skin by iodine fuming, a process that causes the print to be developed like a photograph. Prints on paper are usually recovered by dipping the paper in ninhydrin solution. As the paper dries, the print turns purple and can then be photographed. Prints can also be recovered in the rain. While a rainy scene does not provide the easiest conditions to work under, waiting for the rain to stop could cause us to lose the evidence. Therefore, the print can be sprayed with a small particle reagent such as molybdenum disulfide, commonly called "moly" for short. Moly sticks to the print, which can then be photographed or recovered with fingerprint tape. An umbrella comes in handy during print recovery.

Superglue fuming is another way of recovering prints. It's a technique that was accidentally discovered by a Japanese scientist. The fumes from superglue adhere to prints, coloring them silver gray. In several homicide cases, we actually superglued entire vehicles by tenting them and heating superglue to accelerate the fuming process.

A common superglue tank is nothing more than a glass fish tank with a lid fashioned from hard cardboard. A ceramic light bulb socket—the kind used in storage sheds—is placed in the tank. The electrical cord is extended out of the tank. A 100-watt light bulb is screwed in. A homemade wire frame is fashioned so that it stands above the light bulb. An aluminum foil bowl is placed on the frame above the light bulb. The object to be superglued is placed in the fish tank. (Handguns are usually superglued because they are difficult to

A typical superglue fuming tank

dust.) Superglue is poured into the aluminum foil bowl and the lid placed on the tank and taped shut, creating an airtight container. The light bulb is then plugged into an electrical outlet. The resulting heat from the light bulb causes the superglue to evaporate. The superglue fumes cover all surfaces inside the sealed tank.

A simple experiment you can do at home will show the effect of superglue. First, get a clean glass bottle with a lid, such as a mayonnaise bottle. Form some aluminum foil into a small bowl about one inch in diameter. Place the aluminum foil bowl into the bottom of the mayonnaise jar. Lay a strip of aluminum foil about three inches long by one inch wide on a flat surface. Press your thumb onto the foil strip. (To ensure you have sufficient oils on your thumb, rub it across your forehead or nose before you lay down the print.) Carefully place the foil strip into the bottle. Very carefully drop ten drops or so of any brand of superglue, available at convenience or hardware stores, into the small aluminum foil bowl. (Don't breathe the superglue fumes, which are said to be carcinogenic.) Quickly cover the jar with its lid. Wait an hour. The latent fingerprint will be covered with a grayish-white film, and will be greatly enhanced by the process.

The big problem in Barboza's case was that months after the crime scene investigation, when we identified Tony Williams as Barboza's killer, the fingerprint we recovered didn't match the suspect's inked prints. This was immediately worrisome. We were sure that Barboza's killer was Tony Williams, but the fingerprint of someone else was at the site where the shotgun was fired. Another suspect? Or police contamination? Our thoughts went to the officers who were present. We compared the recovered print with the prints of the field patrol officers who were present, up to the rank of lieutenant. There was no match. We then requested via the administration that ranking officers provide us with their inked prints. The reply we got was distressing. Our request was denied, and we were told not to ask again. The reason seemed obvious to me. The administration did not want to be embarrassed if we learned that the latent fingerprint found at the point where the killer shot the weapon belonged to a ranking police official. We could almost see the headlines: "Police contaminate murder scene with their own fingerprints." So there we were. A suspect in Barboza's murder was in custody, and a critical fingerprint was unidentified. When we went to trial, a defense attorney could create major problems over that issue. Imagine the following scenario.

Defense attorney: "Officer, did you find a fingerprint at the point where the murder weapon was fired?"

Police investigator: "Yes, we did," the answer would have to be.

Defense attorney: "Did it belong to my client, Mr. Williams?"

Police investigator: "No it did not," he would have to answer.

Defense attorney: "Do you know who it belongs to?"

Police investigator: "No, we do not."

The attorney would then turn to the jury and argue that we have the wrong man. That the real killer left his fingerprint at the site of the murder and we failed to identify him.

All conjecture, but all possible with that unidentifiable print. When we went to the prosecutors and explained our dilemma, they told us that if it became an issue at trial, they would ask the court to order that fingerprints of all the officers who were at the crime scene, regardless of rank, be taken and compared with Williams's. It never became an issue at trial, however.

Were we lucky? Or did Williams's defense attorney simply not feel the print was an issue because of all the other evidence we had against him? We won't know for sure, but the fact remains that we cannot afford to contaminate murder crime scenes by carelessly touching things.

By the time we finally got the crime scene to ourselves, we also had some interesting information from the neighbors. Many of the people living around Barboza's house reported hearing two gunshots. This was consistent with other facts we knew. In a planter box next to Barboza's front door were two shotgun-shell casings. After a visual examination of his body, we could see only two wounds: one to the rear of his head and one to his right leg above his knee.

In many murder investigations, the investigating team examines and probes and reenacts the crime, yielding, sometimes, interesting information. In this case, sadness hung over everyone. For some, the tears flowed openly. Others needed time alone. Still others worked on in silence. Each of us dealt with the grim reality of the murder of a fellow police officer in our own way. And perhaps this pall that hung over us dimmed our investigative abilities so that we at first missed what should have been obvious to longtime detectives. It wasn't until we processed the couch that Barboza was lying on that we found a hole in the backrest, torn by a third shotgun blast. The hole in the couch was covered by a blanket—and the blanket was not torn. This raised another question. Who covered the hole with the blanket? We never found out. It would have been understandable for the first officers who responded to the shooting to move a blanket in the shock of the initial discovery, but all of them denied touching it.

Our early speculation was that the suspect entered the room after shooting Barboza to ensure that he was dead. However, there was nothing found at the crime scene to indicate that this had occurred. It also made little sense for the killer to spend more time at the scene, knowing that he woke up the neighborhood and that those neighbors might be calling the police to report the gunshots. We also speculated that the paramedics, while checking Barboza for signs of life, might have moved the blanket. Each of them denied touching the blanket, much less moving it. They were able to pronounce him dead with very little disturbance to his body or the surrounding items on the couch. This brought us back to contamination. Someone obviously moved the blanket, and since no one admitted to it, we had to settle with the thought that a police officer who entered the crime scene inadvertently moved Barboza's blanket. It was, perhaps, unintended contamination, but it caused long hours of concern and misdirected investigation.

So what did we miss that we should have realized from the start? Barboza was killed in the early morning hours. Neighbors reported two gunshots, which they described as occurring about two seconds apart. We found two shotgun-shell casings that flew into the planter box when the shotgun was fired. But we kept missing one important fact.

The neighborhood was asleep.

So what woke them up to hear two shotgun blasts? The first shotgun blast woke them up. And then they heard blasts numbers two and three. Imagine the killer aiming his shotgun at Barboza, who was lying on the couch. Then pulling the trigger. Then engaging the slide, ejecting shell casing number one into the planter box and inserting shotgun shell number two into the chamber. Then pulling the trigger again. Then engaging the slide again and ejecting shell casing number two into the planter box and inserting shotgun shell number three into the chamber. Then pulling the trigger a third time. Only this time, running away, taking the shotgun and shell casing number three—which was still inside the shotgun—with him as he fled.

So the neighbors heard shotgun blasts two and three (number one woke them up), and we found shotgun shell casings one and two. When the neighbors told us they heard two blasts, we should have realized right away that there were actually three blasts, with the first waking the sleeping neighborhood. From now on, when you are awakened from a deep sleep, think about what it was that woke you.

Yet another issue with the investigation was that the neighbors who heard the shotgun blasts also heard, as they described it, a screaming woman. A few quick checks told us that Barboza did have a girlfriend. This raised immediate concerns. Was she there when the killing occurred? Did she flee? If she was there, was she taken by the killer? We grew more concerned when we began to inquire about his girlfriend among Barboza's friends. Several told us that Barboza and another police officer were both interested in the same woman and may have been rivals for her attention. In very private conversations that morning, we discussed the horrific possibility that he was murdered by a rival police officer who then abducted the woman. It was an outrageous thought, but we had to consider every possibility even if it led us where we hoped it would not. It fueled the immediate need to find the woman and the rival cop. We quickly found both. After a few questions, we were able to determine that neither one was involved and eliminate the awful suspicion that the killer could have been a fellow police officer.

A question that arose during the crime-scene investigation was whether Barboza was killed instantly. The medical examiner suggested

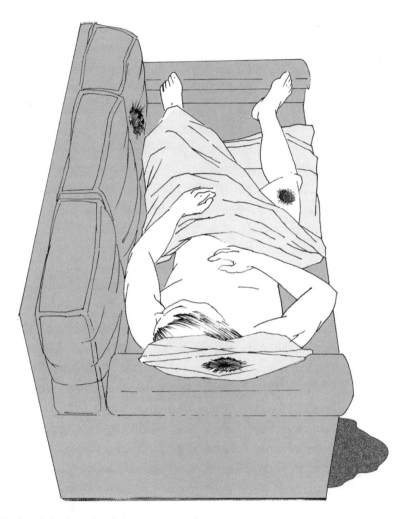

Barboza's body on his living-room couch

that Barboza was shot first in the leg before he was hit by the shot that killed him. We disagreed. In this case, logic prevailed. The first shot struck Barboza in the head, passing first through his pillow. If Barboza had been shot in the leg first, or if the first shot had struck the couch, Barboza would have moved. He would have sat up or rolled over, but he certainly would not have continued to lie on the couch with his head resting quietly on the pillow. If he had sat up first, the secondary blasts would have struck him in the back. Several facts support this. First, neighbors claim that there was about a two-second count between shotgun blasts. Second, a shotgun blast is a very loud explosion. It woke people up all around the neighborhood. Whether the first shot hit him in the leg or missed altogether, Barboza would have awoken and would have been moving. His head would not have been on the pillow when the killing shot was fired. Third, firing a sawed-off shotgun with any accuracy requires careful aim. Once the killer began firing, his ability to aim would have been lost, especially while he was standing and trying to maintain balance on the small tile wall. Barboza must have died instantly with the first shot. This was confirmed later after we developed a suspect.

While it was difficult and painful to work the murder scene, there was still one more task ahead of us that we knew would be solemn and emotional, and which we dreaded: speaking to Troy's parents. Troy was a young man who grew up in a middle-class neighborhood in California. He and his sister were the only children in a family that held a high degree of respect for community and country. When Troy entered the Honolulu Police Department, his parents and sister were very proud of him. And now their only son and brother was dead.

His parents would come from California to claim and bury their son and they would want to speak to the officers who knew him and the detectives who were trying to find his killer. A meeting was arranged in the Criminal Investigation Division's conference room. It was one of the most difficult moments in the years I spent as the lieutenant of the Homicide Detail. When his parents walked in, you could see their emotional strain and grief at facing every parent's nightmare. After the CID major introduced us, Troy's mother walked over and gave us each a hug. Then she stepped back and said through teary eyes, but with a strong voice, "Please find the people who killed our son."

That simple tearful request created almost unimaginable pressure.

Here before us were the heartbroken parents of a young man who died in a community far from home, and who devoted his short life to doing good for that community. How could we face them again if we failed to find his killer? Had we done everything we could possibly do so far in the investigation?

The crime-scene investigation took about two days. We had gathered all the possible evidence and information we could find using all the techniques available to us. But there was nothing at the crime scene that pointed to a particular suspect. Our interviews with family and friends suggested nothing sinister, unlike such interviews in the Kotani murder case, and fellow officers thought that he was killed by someone he arrested. Barboza had made several recent drug arrests, and some thought that revenge was a motive. The flow of information soon dried up. One detective had an innovative idea: shut down Waikīkī.

A haven for our tourists and a symbol of our visitor culture to many, Waikīkī also plays host to prostitutes and drug dealers. The suggestion was to close down all illegal activities in an unprecedented shutdown. In other words, take away the venue for the people who use drugs and prostitution and see what information evolves. It was a good idea because people talk, and the illegal drug network is widespread. We felt confident that information on Barboza's murder was already on the street.

How do you shut down Waikīkī? We called a meeting with the plainclothes Crime Reduction Units of Waikīkī and the bordering patrol areas. It was agreed that the focus for the next few weeks would be prostitution and drug activity in Waikīkī. Prostitutes were included because illicit drugs are part of the lives of many of them. And so it began. The Morals Detail and the Crime Reduction Units would increase their undercover activity and arrest more prostitutes. If we couldn't arrest them for morals offenses, we arrested them for any offense they committed, including jaywalking. We did the same to every drug dealer we could find. And with every arrest came the questioning: "What do you guys know about the murder of the police officer?"

Initial responses were sarcastic, almost smug in reaction to the idea that a cop had been killed. But within a few weeks, attitudes changed. The prostitutes would simply not come out onto the streets. The street drug dealers had no sidewalk to stand on. No street to park their car on. No place to deal their drugs. Everywhere they turned, a cop would be interfering with their illegal ventures. We started to get somewhere.

"Officer, go check with so-and-so, I heard he had some information about the cop who was murdered."

Business was so bad in Waikīkī that the prostitutes were giving us names of the people who supplied them drugs in hopes that we would soon find Barboza's killer. Drug dealers were turning in their friends, partners, and buyers to get us off their backs. Many leads turned up. But nothing firm. Nothing leading to a viable suspect. We needed to crank up the heat. The tone from the officers changed.

"You need to leave Waikīkī and don't come back. And don't go anywhere else, Kapahulu, Kapiʻolani, Hawaiʻi Kai, Waimānalo, we don't care. The island is closed to you. If we catch you, guarantee you hurt big time. We'll take your car, we'll search your house and your parents' house, and we'll take everything that we touch with some help from the forfeiture laws."

So there was some exaggeration, perhaps some excessive bravado, particularly when we knew that we would probably not be successful in seizing anyone's home. But the increased pressure brought in a little more information, and a very important fact emerged from one informant.

"There's a guy dealing from Kāneʻohe, Kahaluʻu area. I heard that he deals with a guy from Los Angeles. I heard that he sold this guy a sawed-off shotgun and three shells. There's talk that this guy from L.A. killed the cop."

That was a first step. It didn't take long to identify the Windward drug dealer. And even less time to convince him that it was in his best interest to be honest with us.

"Oh, yeah, I went sell him the gun. Was one legal gun. The butt and barrel was sawed down, but the length was legal."

"Did you also sell him any ammunition?"

"Oh, yeah. I went sell him three rounds. That's all I had."

"How did you get the gun?"

"Somebody gave me."

"Who?"

"I no remember."

"What was the name of the guy you sold the shotgun to?"

"Oh, I dunno. Somebody told him I have the gun for sale, I guess."

It took a few more minutes to convince our Windward dealer that we would make every effort to put him behind bars for a very long time if he was lying to us.

"Oh yeah, I remember now. His name was Williams. Anthony Williams. From L.A."

"Thank you." Nothing wrong with being polite.

Having this name gave the detectives additional leads to follow up on. Our search had already showed that Williams had been arrested by Barboza for drug offenses. This new information tied his name to the killing. The detectives contacted the Los Angeles Police Department and got more information on the suspect, a small-time hood and drug dealer who bragged about killing people. As we

The mug photograph of Anthony Williams

learned more about him, we learned that he had a friend from L.A. now living in Honolulu who may have been a contact for his drug dealing.

We quickly found his friend. At first this man was very reluctant to comment, but when he realized that he was facing possible accomplice charges, he chose to tell us what he knew.

Williams had confided in him that during a court hearing in Honolulu, he found Barboza's name and address in a phone book and decided that if he killed Barboza, there would be no witnesses against him in court. He bought a shotgun and three shotgun shells from someone he knew and went to Barboza's house late one night. He waited alongside the house because he thought that Barboza was still at work. He waited and waited and thought that Barboza had gone out after work because it was now early morning. Suddenly a light came on in the bathroom, and he realized that Barboza was actually at home. He walked to the patio and watched Barboza go back to the couch and lie down. He aimed the shotgun and shot the cop three times. Williams told his friend that he was screaming as he shot the cop. Then he ran from the house, figuring that cops would be on their way. Williams went back to Waikīkī and threw the shotgun into the Ala Wai Canal. Later he caught a cab to the airport and went home to Los Angeles. The killer himself told a friend what we had surmised from the evidence: the cop was awake when he was murdered.

Everything fit. Motive, weapon, and the method of the killing. We had our suspect. A little more investigation turned up information that Williams dealt drugs with a local dealer. Detectives approached him, and he soon agreed to work with us to bring Williams back to Honolulu. The local dealer made a call. They would trade drugs and money. A date was set for Williams to come to Hawai'i. Working with the L.A. detectives, we were informed that Williams was on a plane and on his way to Honolulu. We picked up the tail at the airport and followed him to the local dealer's apartment, where a team of officers waited. He was greeted by the local dealer and entered the trap.

Sitting in the living room, prior to the drug deal, Williams told the local dealer about Barboza's murder. All of it was recorded on a hidden tape. The deal was consummated. Williams walked into the hall and was arrested. There was more than one detective waiting in that hallway hoping that Williams would pull a gun on them.

He was charged with murder in the first degree, an offense reserved for the people who kill police officers, judges, prosecutors, multiple victims, and the very young or the elderly, and for murder-for-hire cases. We had special security at his trial, where the judge agreed to keep him handcuffed and shackled due to his violent nature, his association with Los Angeles gang members, and a threat passed to us that his associates might try to free him from custody.

Tony Williams was convicted of first-degree murder and sentenced to life in prison without the possibility of parole.

Troy Barboza is remembered each year in the Law Enforcement Torch Run that carries his name and raises money and public awareness about children involved in Special Olympics as it honors the young police officer who once coached them.

And in honoring him, they honor the parents and family who lost their only son and brother in the line of duty to HPD and the people of Honolulu.

14

The Shooting of Officer Stan Cook

Think about what you'd be prepared to risk your life for: to protect your family, serve your country? Noble reasons with strong emotional attachments. But how about teasing a stranger about his big ears?

Norman Norman, Jr., and his brother, Fred Norman, ended up dead after they made fun of the big ears of a tall man named Juan Velasquez at Jack in the Box in Waikīkī. The brothers were out on the town with their dates and stopped to buy some fast food late that summer night in 1991. When they started picking on the stranger, the stranger got irritated, then got angry, then got a gun. He shot and killed them both. Police tracked down the killer, whose defense first claimed that he heard spirits and should be acquitted because he was insane. A mistrial was declared in 1993, and it took another trial the following year to convict Velasquez of the double murder. He was sent to prison and so was his wife, Carmen Sevilla, who as his accomplice provided him with the gun he used that night. Velasquez and his ex-wife were convicted of murder, and justice was served. But the Norman brothers were dead from a confrontation that began simply enough as a smart-aleck remark about a stranger's ears.

How about spilling a beer?

A group of men were drinking one night outside a sausage factory on Puʻuhale Road in Kalihi. They'd had a few. Then a few more. Another man drove into the parking lot where they were drinking and knocked over an open beer. An argument began, and one of the drinkers pulled out a gun to end it. That party ended with a spilled beer and a dead man.

Or how about getting into a snit over the way your neighbor drives his car?

That was the case in the Punchbowl area, where one man thought his neighbor drove too close to him as he was heading into the lane to park his car. The man standing on the roadside began to shout. The driver got out of his car, they fought, and the man who started the fight got knocked down. As he fell, he hit his head on a curb and died. But he got to make that one last point to his neighbor. A point that ended in a manslaughter conviction.

In the case in which Officer Stan Cook was shot, John Sinapati was trying to avoid arrest for the batu—a.k.a. ice, but scientifically known as crystal methamphetamine—that he had hidden in his car. He also had hidden an AK-47 rifle. Cook survived, but Sinapati made the trip to the morgue.

With an average of about forty murders a year occurring in Honolulu, homicide detectives inevitably handle a few cases in which the motives are incredibly hard to believe. How do we define "motive"? It's the underlying reason for the actions a person takes in committing an offense. Most motives arise from some form of argument between two people who know each other fairly well. An example of this is a domestic or family quarrel. Other motives are sexually related, such as those in serial killings or sexual homicides. Many crimes involve drugs: people high on drugs killing each other, people angry because they want the drugs someone else has or because they haven't been paid for drugs that they delivered. The drug that appears most in such cases is ice. And there are organized crime–related killings or those in which someone puts out a contract to have another person killed. You don't have to belong to a crime family to do that.

In one case, a marine didn't want to be married to his wife anymore, so he hired two other marines to get his wife drunk and kill her. Because she frequented bars with her husband and the men hired to kill her, it wasn't difficult to get her to go out with them. They went drinking in Honolulu and as they drove back to the Windward side with the woman sitting between the two men, the marine in the passenger seat, fueled by adrenaline, shouted out, punched the woman in the throat, then strangled her with his hands—all while a police officer drove behind them. The officer tried to pull the suspects over with his siren and blue light, but the attack continued until the woman was dead. Besides the killer and his accomplice, the woman's husband was also convicted of murder.

During the late 1980s and early 1990s, Honolulu saw the number of murders connected to ice skyrocket. Sometimes the killer was on ice, sometimes the killer and the victim were on ice, and sometimes the killing occurred over the theft of ice. Drugs and murders are no strangers to any community, but the link between that particular drug and violent death shot up out of nowhere as a significant contributing factor in killings during those years.

Ice does very bad things to people. Not only is it a highly addictive drug, but its continued use makes people more aggressive and more violent. A man high on ice got into an argument with his wife at their Whitmore Village home. Then he killed her, strangling her with an electrical cord from an appliance, wrapping and tying it extraordinarily tightly around her neck—so tightly that the furrow left by the cord was nearly an inch deep. Then he took a knife and stabbed her repeatedly in the face. He fled the scene before officers arrived. His wife was unrecognizable when we arrived at her residence to begin the investigation.

Her husband called the crime scene while we were there. He told us that he was coming back to kill us. Of course we invited him to return, never expecting him to do so. But since he was really high on ice, he actually came back. A chase ensued. Beat officers who were protecting the scene for us chased the suspect from Whitmore Village through Wahiawā to Kunia Road to ʻEwa Beach, where he crashed his car. He was arrested, but it was a full day before he was sober enough for investigators to speak to him. He denied killing his wife, claiming that he had no memory of the incident. Nevertheless, he was charged and convicted of his wife's murder.

Stan Cook, a solo motorcycle officer, stopped a vehicle in Waipahu for a traffic citation on August 31, 1994, at 8:35 in the morning. He stopped the car because he thought the license plate was fraudulent. Cook didn't know that the driver, John Sinapati, had a cache of crystal methamphetamine and a loaded AK-47 rifle hidden under a blue jacket on the front seat.

After getting Sinapati's license and making a check with police dispatch, Cook returned to the vehicle, checked the license plate, and then walked back to the driver's window. While informing Sinapati that he was going to issue a citation, he noticed the blue jacket with something under it. As he asked to see what was under the jacket, Sinapati grabbed the rifle.

Cook drew his weapon and tried to retreat to a safe position behind the car. But it was too late. The suspect was shooting at him. Cook fired several rounds through the back window of the car.

There was one giant stroke of luck in Cook's favor: one of his bullets struck the suspect in the spine, paralyzing him. The best the suspect could do at that moment was to lean out the window. As

The body of John Sinapati after the shootout with Officer Stan Cook

Cook tried to get back to his motorcycle, Sinapati shot him several times. Cook fell backward and continued to fire at Sinapati, who was leaning out the driver's window and firing at Cook. Cook was shot several more times as he lay on the ground, but his training saved his life. He maintained his concentration and accurately returned fire toward the man trying to kill him. After emptying his clip, Cook reloaded and continued firing. In a few more seconds it was over. Cook lay on the pavement seriously wounded, and Sinapati hung dead from the car window, a pool of blood collecting beneath his head. Cook crawled to his motorcycle and called police dispatch. In a few more minutes, he was on his way to the hospital. Sinapati was on his way to the morgue.

⊕

Firearms are generally categorized into two groups: shoulder firearms, such as rifles and shotguns; and handguns, such as revolvers and pistols. They can be further categorized as smoothbore or rifled weapons.

Rifling is a series of spiral channels cut into the barrel that give the bullet a twisting motion when it's fired to stabilize it as it leaves the barrel. The channels and raised surfaces of a rifled barrel are called "grooves" and "lands" respectively. The caliber of a rifled weapon, measured in millimeters or hundredths or thousandths of an inch, is the diameter of the bore measured between two opposite lands.

Ammunition is categorized into two types: rimfire and centerfire, referring to the primer located in the base of the cartridge. The term "bullet" is defined as the projectile fired from the weapon. It is made of a lead alloy and can be nonjacketed, jacketed, or semijacketed with copper or brass. The purpose of the jacket is to keep the bullet intact as much as possible when it strikes an object.

A number of forensic tests can be performed on weapons or ammunition when firearms used in murder cases are recovered. These tests include

- Operability. Some laws require that a gun be in working order for it to be classified as a weapon.

- Distance determination. The weapon is fired at a piece of white paper and the stippling patterns recorded. "Stippling" is the proper term for the commonly misused term "powder burns." The patterns are then compared with those recovered as evidence, such as the stippling on a victim's clothing.

- Velocity. Velocity is determined by firing the bullet through two magnetic fields that are set apart at a measured specific distance.

As the bullet passes the first magnetic field, a timer starts. When it passes the second magnetic field, the timer stops. The speed of the bullet can then be computed.

- Bullet striations. Evidence from a bullet recovered from a victim can be compared against a test sample to determine if the bullets were fired from the same weapon.

- Gunshot residue (GSR). GSR occurs when a firearm is discharged. Particles of unburned powder from the primer fall onto the hand of the shooter. The hand can be processed and evidence examined under a scanning electron microscope. That's why you'll sometimes see suspects in a shooting in custody wearing paper bags over their hands to protect possible evidence.

At crime scenes where cartridges are strewn about, care must be taken to prevent damaging the evidence by driving over or stepping on them. This sounds obvious, but because investigators at the scene are responsible for supervising many different activities at the scene at the same time, evidence is sometimes damaged.

In some cases, people unintentionally kill others. At Zippy's Waimalu one night, Benjamin Chi, a martial arts expert, got into a fight. Chi kicked the victim in the chest near his heart, and the victim died. When someone is killed, people usually come forward and tell us what a wonderful person the victim was, but in this case, a number of people came forward to describe the suspect as a caring, responsible person unlikely to pick fights. His supporters believed he was not the aggressor but ended up killing someone as he defended himself. Either way, it was clear that he had not started the evening intending to take another life or even believing he would be in a fight.

Sometimes, murders come out of misunderstandings—scary and horrifying misunderstandings. A young woman named Eyvette Maelega, who lived with her family in a housing project in Kalihi, was strangled by her husband. Her mother and stepfather heard Muao Maelega arguing with Eyvette behind a closed door, which he barricaded, but they were too afraid to intervene. When the argument ended, Eyvette was dead, strangled with the cord to a clock radio. This was a tragically common domestic argument, leaving an infant without a mother. But the really chilling part about this case was revealed when the detectives interviewing the suspect learned the cause of his fatal fury. After the recent delivery of the Maelegas' baby, the doctor described to the husband how many centimeters his wife's cervix had dilated. Somehow, through a language and cultural barrier, Muao misinterpreted the doctor's remark as a comment about penis size, and since he did not consider himself to measure up to what he was hearing, he concluded that his wife was having an affair with someone else. Since he and his wife lived with only one other man, he believed that she must be having an affair with her stepfather. That suspicion ate at him until the fatal night, even though there was no basis for his jealous rage.

Murders happen for countless reasons—some of them ridiculous, all of them sad. Part of the investigator's job is to determine what the killer's motive was. It's tragic to think that a man would kill his wife because he misunderstood a medical term, or that someone would try to kill a police officer because of a traffic ticket. And it's sobering to realize how even trivial incidents can lead to murder and ruin so many lives.

15
The Killing of Dana Ambrose

Dana Ambrose, a nineteen-year-old Leeward Community College student, was putting herself through school with a job as a waitress at Brew Moon, a microbrewery restaurant near Waikīkī. She lived in Haleʻiwa on Oʻahu's North Shore, and the night she died, October 7, 2000, she was headed home from work. Friends and family describe her as a sweet, friendly young woman who had just proudly announced she had won an art scholarship to the University of Hawaiʻi.

She was headed toward the North Shore on School Street and had just entered the intersection at Pali Highway when her 2000 Honda Civic was broadsided by a 1993 Ford Thunderbird speeding through the red light. The Thunderbird was driven by police officer Clyde Arakawa. Ambrose was killed instantly.

Arakawa, a veteran police officer with enough years on the force to retire, had a reputation: he was a drinker who had gotten in trouble for his intoxicated behavior before. Now he found himself facing a charge of negligent homicide.

Amazingly, many people don't consider negligent homicides serious death cases. How can a death case not be serious? After all, even though the term "murder" isn't used, someone lost his or her life because of the actions of another person. But some people argue that that person acted negligently, making the death "accidental." The person didn't intend any harm. But if it's accidental, why is it a crime?

Murder, manslaughter, and negligent homicide are types of

homicide that are defined in part on the defendant's state of mind. Murder is an offense that requires an intentional and knowing state of mind, while manslaughter requires a reckless state of mind. Negligent homicide involves the taking of life while in operation of a motor vehicle and requires a negligent state of mind.

"State of mind" is one of the elements of the *corpus delicti,* or body of the crime. Three primary elements make up the *corpus delicti.* The first is a*ctus reus,* or the guilty act—the act of the crime itself. Second is *mens rea,* the guilty mind—the defendant's state of mind at the time of the act. Last comes the need for *concurrence,* having *actus reus* and *mens rea* occurring simultaneously. With all three elements, the *corpus delicti* is satisfied.

In discussing *mens rea,* the penal code description of a criminal offense describes four states of mind: Stated simply, they are, in descending order of severity:

Intentional, or having a *conscious object,* that your actions would cause a specific harm.

Knowing, or *being aware* that your actions would cause a specific harm.

Reckless, or having a *conscious disregard* that your actions would cause a specific harm.

Negligent, or when you *should have been aware* that your actions would cause a specific harm.

The crime of negligent homicide is investigated with the same intensity as a murder, but Traffic Division investigators often fight an uphill battle when they investigate a traffic-related death. For one thing, the suspect in a negligent homicide investigation is usually still at the scene or in the hospital. For another, unlike the general homicide investigation, the negligent homicide case tends to be extraordinarily technical. Investigators must learn to use instruments similar to those used by surveyors to get absolute distances. They must understand advanced mathematics to calculate speed from tire skid marks, or to determine speed by the degree of crush to a vehicle. Like murder investigators, they must use their skills to examine fine details to learn if lights were on, if brakes were applied, or what happened to the vehicle after the crash.

Sadly, the negligent homicide investigator doesn't get as much respect as the homicide investigator in spite of his or her expertise. After all, it was just an accident—as some people in the community put it. During my assignment as the major in charge of the Traffic Division, an officer told me that he thought lawmakers created this crime of homicide with a state of mind based on negligence because driving is part of the American culture and people shouldn't be penalized too severely just because someone got killed while they were driving a car. He was being sarcastic during a moment of frustration because the prosecutor's office declined to charge a suspect with manslaughter, choosing instead to charge negligent homicide. The accused was drunk and speeding and someone died because of that.

A negligent homicide charge is easier to prosecute successfully than a charge of manslaughter. Defendants often plead guilty. Prosecutors allow those drivers to plead guilty to a lesser charge as part of a plea agreement. The cases take less time and effort that way. As recently as the late 1990s, the majority of people convicted in felony negligent homicide cases received little jail time. The consequences for killing someone with a car were not that serious. Sure, the driver lost his license and had to attend classes on driving or alcohol abuse, and perhaps he even did some months in jail or community service. But the punishment for that offense didn't seem to match the severity of the crime.

In the Ambrose case, Arakawa was a police officer who was found to be intoxicated. That means he chose to drink and then he chose to drive. He drank until he got drunk. That was an intentional act, wasn't it? Then he got into his car and drove. He was still doing something intentionally. He meant to drink and he still decided to drive. And while he was driving, he decided to speed. Think back to the description of legal states of mind. Recklessness: a conscious disregard of the risk that your actions would cause a specific harm. That definition seems to fit better than negligence, when the defendant *should have known.*

Arakawa's drinking had caused him to make the news once before. In 1992, Arakawa, drunk, went into a stranger's Kailua home and fell asleep on the couch, thinking he'd entered his own home. The woman who lived there called the police, who found him to have a blood alcohol content of twice the legal limit.

The jury in the Ambrose case seemed to agree with the prosecution that Arakawa was a drunk driver in spite of Arakawa's claim that he had a "practiced liver" that processed alcohol better than yours or mine, or ours put together. Bottom line: people—police officers included—should not be driving drunk. Period. If anything, people expect a police officer to have a fairly good idea that drinking eleven beers before getting behind the wheel is more than just a mistake.

Here are a couple of definitions from the Hawai'i penal code:

> §707-702 Manslaughter. (1) A person commits the offense of manslaughter if:
> (a) He recklessly causes the death of another person; or
> (b) He intentionally causes another person to commit suicide.

> [§707-702.5] Negligent homicide in the first degree. (1) A person is guilty of the offense of negligent homicide in the first degree if that person causes the death of another person by the operation of a vehicle in a negligent manner while under the influence of drugs or alcohol.

When a speeding drunk driver kills an innocent person, police officers try to convince prosecutors that these people were reckless, not negligent. If you drink until you're drunk and you speed and you kill another person, you should be guilty of manslaughter, not negligent homicide. Negligent homicide should be reserved for the driver not paying attention—or even the driver who falls asleep at the wheel—who causes a collision that kills someone.

What prosecutors often tell us is that if more than one person was killed, they would consider manslaughter over negligent homicide because the act was more grievous. But there's nothing in the penal code definitions of manslaughter and negligent homicide that states that the deaths of two or more people are more serious or grievous than the death of one person. Most people agree that a speeding drunk who takes one life rather than two in a collision is guilty of a serious offense. The speeding drunk who kills two can be charged with the serious offense twice to fit that crime.

The mug photograph of Clyde Arakawa

The city prosecutor's office did bring manslaughter charges against Clyde Arakawa in 2001. But an article in *The Honolulu Advertiser* on April 4, 2002, quotes City Prosecutor Peter Carlisle as saying: "We are going to consider prior alcohol-related offenses, which could be like an [Clyde] Arakawa breaking into a house when you're stuporously drunk or a prior DUI and having that raise the bar from negligent homicide . . . to manslaughter."

Isn't this bringing a separate factor into the equation? If you drink and drive and speed and kill someone, but you don't have a history of alcohol-related offenses, we'll give you a break and charge you with the lesser crime of negligent homicide. If you have a prior alcohol-related offense, we're throwing the book at you.

Doesn't this reflect society's laissez-faire attitude toward drinking and driving? Doesn't this do an injustice to the victims and their families?

When we add this factor of prior alcohol-related offenses, we are failing to consider that people still lose their lives under the same circumstances and conditions: drunkenness, driving, and speed, regardless of the defendant's past criminal history. Would it not be more equitable for the victims and their families if any defendant who kills a person while speeding and driving drunk be charged with manslaughter and not negligent homicide? *And*, if a defendant has a prior alcohol-related offense, then shouldn't that defendant be eligible for an extended sentence beyond the twenty years mandated by the penal code? We could then say that we are treating victims, their families, *and* the defendants with equity when we charge offenders who drink and drive and speed and kill. Makes sense to me.

The Clyde Arakawa case, a prime example of DUI-related killings, jumped into the limelight instantly because of several factors. First, Arakawa was an off-duty police officer at the time he killed Dana Ambrose. Second, the crime-scene investigators did not treat Arakawa the way they would have treated a suspect who was not a police officer. Nor did they treat the crime scene, where the killing occurred, in the same manner that they would have if the suspect was not a police officer. And yes, the intersection of School Street and Pali Highway where those two cars lay twisted and mangled was a crime scene. Arakawa was allowed to remain inside the crime scene. Arakawa was allowed to call his attorney and have that attorney come to the crime scene. Another suspect would have been handcuffed, taken to the police cellblock, and booked.

Did those investigators deliberately try to cover up for Arakawa?

Did they deliberately try to manipulate evidence in his favor? No, I don't think that was the case at all. However, they did give him unprecedented freedom to walk around the crime scene. They let him bring in his attorney to view the very evidence that the police go through extraordinary efforts to protect from defense eyes. That evidence needs to be protected until the investigators have the opportunity to record, examine, and conduct tests on it.

What the community saw was police investigators who appeared to be giving special treatment to a suspect in a killing. What the community didn't see was that they were faced with a suspect who was also a fellow police officer, someone they had known for decades and were uncomfortable treating as they would any other suspect.

A critical reality exists here. Police officers, perhaps more so than members of most other professions, succumb to the stress of being part of a *brotherhood*. That goes beyond the camaraderie felt in many walks of life. In everyday police work, when one officer needs lifesaving help, another officer is expected to put his own life in jeopardy to help the one in trouble. Even if the two dislike each other. That's how intense this *brotherhood* can be. Police officers tend to feel alone in the world. It's us against everyone else. If I can't depend on my fellow police officers to help me, then who? This is known as the "Custer Syndrome": officers feel surrounded by adversity and must band together to maintain their security.

In the Arakawa case the officers on the scene had an obligation to treat Arakawa no differently than they would any other citizen in the same circumstance. Even though they did not let him get away or damage evidence against himself, the public was left with the image of police officers comforting the suspect at the crime scene he created. And that was damaging to the police image even if it didn't hamper the investigation or conviction.

When I spoke to some of the officers who conducted the Arakawa investigation, it became apparent that there truly was no intent on their part to prejudice the case. But they acknowledged that, under very stressful conditions, they did make mistakes.

Another aspect of the Arakawa case proved to be of concern. Police administrators were too slow to comment about what the community saw and heard on television—that officers at the scene appeared to be allowing unusual courtesies to the suspect in a death case because that suspect was a police officer. The battle between the media's claim of the public's right to know and the police need for confidentiality in criminal investigations took center stage in Arakawa's case. The key difference here was that the media were not so much looking for information on the investigation as for answers to why a police officer was treated differently by the police investigators. It simply wasn't right that Arakawa was allowed to stroll around the crime scene, where he had caused a death, and the media weren't to blame for photographing the scene. Many people agree that Honolulu police chief Lee Donohue or some other ranking official should have addressed this issue with the community immediately. The public impression of improper actions or police cover-up began to pop up in discussions all over town.

It was nonsense for police administrators to say they were waiting for the investigation to conclude or they didn't want to taint evidence or they couldn't speak because the internal investigation had just begun or they were preventing any misunderstanding that might be caused by speaking prematurely. They could have shown a total commitment to impartiality if they had immediately acknowledged that they made a mistake and that the improprieties were being investigated. Days later, Donohue publicly acknowledged that "courtesies" were shown to Arakawa. But the image of police officers doing wrong was already emblazoned in the minds of many, some of whom called for Donohue to resign.

The police learned lessons from this tragedy. One is that the police are no different from the people they are sworn to protect, and when officers are suspected of breaking the law, they should be treated exactly the same as civilians. Another is that police administrators should provide training to help officers deal with the stressful peer pressure placed on officers who investigate fellow officers. Finally, the community needs to hear from police officials as quickly as possible when police officers are suspected of committing crimes. This is an important aspect of the police-community alliance.

In January of 2002, days before Arakawa's trial began, *The Honolulu Advertiser* reported that the police union said six officers were disciplined in relation to that special treatment. The trial, however, showed that the investigators actually did a professional job in their investigation, as the evidence they documented and presented in court proved damning to Arakawa's claim that Dana Ambrose was speeding and ran the red light. It was satisfying to learn that even if some officers didn't follow proper protocol in handling the suspect, they did investigate Arakawa's crime thoroughly and came to the proper conclusion.

Communication remains extremely important. Silence, in these circumstances, breeds suspicion. Thankfully, we see yet again that police officers who commit crimes will be called upon to be accountable for their actions.

Not every traffic death involves the negligent or reckless action of another person. In 1974, I was working as a patrol officer in the Kāne'ohe District. Late one midnight shift I was driving up the Likelike Highway when I saw a Volkswagen bug speeding down the highway with its lights off. I sped up to the tunnels and turned back down toward Kāne'ohe. By the time I reached Kahekili Highway, the Volkswagen was gone. I had two choices: proceed straight toward Kāne'ohe Bay Drive or turn left onto Kahekili Highway. I headed down Kahekili. When I reached He'eia Road, I saw the VW. It was far ahead of me, going in the Kahuku direction, its lights still off. But the danger had increased tremendously. It was speeding down the highway on the wrong side of the road. I accelerated after it, but as it reached the top of the distant hill I saw a pair of bright headlights appear for an instant. They were coming toward me.

The collision was like an explosion. There was a bright burst, just for an instant, then a cloud of debris. I radioed the station that there had been a head-on collision and gave the location. In seconds I was at the scene, but there was only the mangled frame of the VW bug on the roadway. I got out of my car and only then saw the broken guardrail and the hole in the brush at the side of the road. I looked down and saw a large white truck lying on its side about twenty feet down the embankment. The driver had climbed up from the ravine, and I helped him onto the flat roadway surface. He was shaken but appeared to be physically unhurt. He spoke to me as we walked to the Volkswagen.

"Officer, the Volkswagen was in my lane. I didn't see it until the last second. I tried to swerve but . . ."

He stopped speaking, because what had once been a hardtop sedan was now without a roof. In his heavy truck, he had run right over the bug just before he crashed through the guardrail and into the ravine. We could see a woman in the driver's seat. The seat back was pushed flat, so that she was lying down on it. I approached her, but in the dark, even with my flashlight, could not make out the types of injuries she had. The truck driver stayed about ten feet behind me. We could see lots of blood.

The woman was dressed in dark clothing and had long dark hair that covered her face and shoulders. I touched her wrist and felt for a pulse. Nothing. I reached my hand through her hair to her neck, again looking for a pulse, and my fingers touched warm liquid. I brushed her hair away to see what her injury was. The next moment was horrifying. The woman's head slid down her shoulders onto her chest. Her head was crushed, and she had been partially decapitated when she crashed into the truck.

Why I did what I did next I have never been able to exactly understand. I grabbed her head and placed it back on her shoulders in the position it was when I first saw her. I've thought about this many times, and the only explanation I can come up with is that I was so shocked at seeing her crushed head slide down to her chest that I subconsciously needed to put it back in its normal position. A thought kept returning to me for a long time afterward: for its size, her head seemed very heavy.

With all the traumatic events and violent incidents that I was involved in during my career with HPD, this one ranks at the top, along with the Kaka'ako sniper incident described in *Honolulu Cop*.

Many years later, I came to realize that even though the woman suffered the greatest loss, that of her life in that terrible crash, the truck driver and I were also trauma victims. For him, being part of the crash and, for both of us, witnessing the aftermath and her severe head injuries made us victims as well. I don't know what happened to that truck driver, but the woman's death remains with me to this day.

For Dana Ambrose's family, their grief will be life long. The civil suit they filed against the city and Arakawa will not bring their daughter back, no matter what the result, nor ease the pain they feel.

When people drive, they must remember the responsibility they take on for their passengers, other drivers, pedestrians, and themselves. There are consequences. Clyde Arakawa was sentenced to twenty years in prison. And the Hawai'i Paroling Authority determined he must serve a minimum of eight years before he is eligible for parole.

He'll be sixty-eight years old.

16
The Murders of Lisa Au and Diane Suzuki

Who killed Lisa Au? And who killed Diane Suzuki? But wait, is Diane Suzuki really dead? Not according to some people. They swear they saw her at Disneyland. Many people insist they saw her in Tokyo. It all comes down to what you believe. And that is exactly why neither case has been brought to trial.

In January of 1982, a nineteen-year-old Kailua woman named Lisa Au disappeared on a rainy Thursday night. Her car was found the next morning alongside Kalaniana'ole Highway, near the old Kailua Drive-In theater. It appeared she was headed for her home in Kailua after eating homemade enchiladas for dinner in town with friends. For some reason she stopped. Some people believe she was pulled over by a police officer. Others believe that her car was planted there and that she was murdered elsewhere. Still, she was gone.

Diane Suzuki's was a case with a very different story. Diane was a young woman who taught dance for the Rosalie Woodson Dance Studio in 'Aiea. In July of 1985, Diane and her friends had planned a weekend getaway. Diane was going to finish the dance class she was teaching, jump in the car, and spend the weekend relaxing with her friends. She never got to the car. Some people believe that a man in a Volkswagen abducted her. Others believe that she was murdered in the dance studio where she worked. Still others believe that she simply walked away from the people in her life.

So why are both of these cases still unsolved? Simple. It has to do with direct vs. circumstantial evidence.

The prosecuting attorney does not believe there is sufficient *direct evidence* to convict anyone in either case. Direct evidence? That means evidence that directly proves a fact. For example: A person is shot to death. A bullet is recovered from the body during autopsy. A suspect is arrested with a handgun in his possession. The handgun is test-fired and the test-fire sample is compared with the bullet recovered from the body. There is a positive match. What's the direct evidence? Only that the bullet recovered from the dead person's body was fired from the handgun recovered from the suspect. It does not prove that the suspect pulled the trigger.

So is that it? Is that the only way we can prove things in court? Of course not. Evidence can vary greatly. There are two basic types of evidence: *physical evidence*, or that which has breadth, width, and depth—in other words, anything we can touch; and *testimonial evidence*—witness statements and confessions. Both of these categories can include direct evidence.

But if the criminal justice system depended only on direct evidence to convict criminals, we wouldn't get many convictions. We often have to rely on *circumstantial evidence*, that is, evidence that requires interpretation.

Both physical and testimonial evidence can be circumstantial, requiring interpretation. Interpretation by whom? The jury or the judge. Although various detectives in the Lisa Au and Diane Suzuki murders and again in the serial killings in Honolulu have argued that there actually *is* enough circumstantial evidence to take all these cases to trial, there's the risk, with circumstantial evidence, that the judge or jury will interpret the evidence in favor of the defendant. And that's the underlying reason that the suspects in the murders of Lisa Au, Diane Suzuki, and the serial killings have never gone to trial, and probably never will.

To convince the judge or jury, the prosecutor must work hard to prove to the judge or jury that his or her interpretation of the circumstantial evidence is the right one. Work hard? Yes, using logic, discussion, judgment, persuasion, and arguments. And many detectives think the difficulty of the task affects the types of cases the prosecutors take to court. They think that some prosecutors need a great deal of direct evidence before they accept a case. The detectives say that those prosecutors need a "silver platter." What they mean by this is that the case itself will convict the defendant—with the prosecutor having to do little more than present the items of evidence one after another.

On the other hand, there's some good prosecutorial logic involved in not risking a case. If a prosecutor takes a case to court with substantial circumstantial evidence but limited direct evidence and loses, the defendant goes free. The counterargument is that as long as the defendant has not been charged with the offense, he's out of prison and free anyway, so why not prosecute? How long does one wait for a piece of direct evidence to appear?

"Sometimes you have to have the patience of a mountain." This statement was made to me by Wes Kan, a deputy prosecuting attorney whom I consulted regarding the Kāhala Panty Burglar case. I was venting because we had so little information to go on, and I valued Wes's opinion.

The patience of a mountain. What he meant by that was that some investigations unfold slowly. There are some investigations that lead nowhere, that run into dead ends. There are some cases that end up on some shelf sitting and waiting for something to happen.

And in some cases, things do happen. New investigative techniques are developed and investigators get an opportunity to go back to the scene. This happened in both the Diane Suzuki missing-person case and in the serial killings that plagued Honolulu in the mid-1980s. Luminol was developed and used as an investigative tool, and in both cases we were able to obtain search warrants and go back in time, if you will, to look for more evidence.

Additional witnesses may develop, or suspects may have pangs of conscience and decide to turn themselves in. It's highly unlikely that after fifteen years another witness is going to show up in the Diane Suzuki murder or that her killer will decide to confess. But it's been said in some scientific circles that if you wait long enough, anything can happen.

Just what does "if you wait long enough" mean? "Wait" is a

four-letter word to many investigators. A case sitting on a shelf is not going to solve itself. Usually, new direct evidence is not going to show up by itself, either. Usually, all the direct evidence we have when we're considering a case is all we're ever going to get. Usually, the memory of witnesses fades or the witnesses die if we wait too long. At some point, a decision needs to be made. Do we let the case sit and wait? Or do we prosecute and attempt to convince the jury through the circumstantial evidence that the suspect is guilty? Do we let the killer get away with murder? Or do we at least try to convict? New witnesses have developed and suspects have confessed in various jurisdictions on rare occasions. And because it's possible that it *could* happen, we have to protect the investigation and the evidence.

But that doesn't mean we have to like the wait. It doesn't mean that we agree that we should wait. In both the serial killings and Diane Suzuki's disappearance, investigators thought there was enough evidence to arrest and charge the people responsible for those murders *and* win the case. Everyone who investigated Diane Suzuki's disappearance believes she was murdered. However, the criminal justice system does not allow cops to play judge and jury. The prosecutors have the responsibility of charging and trying the accused, and their goal is to win the case—regardless of what the police think.

So in those cases in which a murder suspect has not been charged, the police need to be patient and protect the investigation and the evidence. It doesn't mean we don't know who the murderer is.

Part of the effort to protect the investigation and evidence is to not reveal information critical to the case. And in this book we have considered the possibility that those cases could be reopened and we have therefore not disclosed crucial details that could hamper the prosecution. The same is true for names and places. Whenever necessary, we have taken precautions to protect identities and locations.

It's hard not to get emotional about cases with good circumstantial evidence remaining unsolved. Or when we think of a killer enjoying his life after taking the life of another. Or when we learn that the parents of a murder victim have died without seeing the killer of their child brought to justice, sometimes without even being able to bury their loved one or know for certain that he or she is dead. Would those parents have said, "No, let the case sit, wait until more evidence or another witness shows up because we don't want to lose"? Or would they have said, "Why is the murderer of my child still free? Let's try. If we fail, then he remains free—as he is right now. But if there's a possibility that we could convict, let's try. Maybe another family will be spared that horrible loss if we try."

So what about the cases? Should they still be sitting on a shelf?

Lisa Au was pretty and pleasant, and she knew a lot of people in the Windward community through her job as a hair stylist at a Kailua salon. Wherever we went we found someone who worked with her, went to school with her, or knew the family. She wasn't flashy or famous, and that very fact made the crime hit home for many people.

It also was a crime that touched many because of its ordinary elements. Lisa was driving on a busy stretch of highway traveled daily by thousands of commuters. She left Honolulu for the Windward side before midnight. Nothing about her life or her behavior that night seemed especially risky or potentially dangerous. How many other young women thought it could have been them in a car at night, facing an unexpected threat alone? How many parents started to keep closer tabs on their teenagers and young adult children?

When her car was discovered, her purse, car keys, and some money were on the seat. But her driver's license and car registration were missing. Police eventually disclosed reports that someone dressed like a police officer had been stopping lone women drivers at night. Those facts heightened the tension, making the community suspicious of the police. The folks that they were supposed to turn to for help suddenly fell into the suspect category. Adding to the suspicion were reports from several people who said they thought they saw a police car stopped behind Lisa's vehicle—not the department's blue-and-white vehicle, but the privately owned type that most of the officers drove at that time.

About ten days after Lisa's car was discovered, a man walking his dog on Tantalus found Lisa's body in the brush off the roadway. The investigation focused on the possibility that a police officer was her killer. The investigation also focused on Lisa's friends. Ultimately, there was just not enough evidence, either direct or circumstantial, to convince prosecutors to bring charges against anyone.

But the HPD administration *was* concerned enough to outlaw blue lights in the grills of police officers' vehicles. Prior to Lisa's case, motorized police officers—who are authorized to operate their own vehicles—could have these blue lights installed. For some officers, this was a fun thing. They would go out and buy the blue lights and the blinkers that would cause the lights to flash in as fancy a sequence as the officers could think of. Grill lights allowed the officers to pull over cars even when they were off duty. The grill lights and siren were an accepted tool for the police, and people would comply when an off-duty police officer pulled them over. Until Lisa was killed.

With her murder, and the suspicion that a police officer pulled her over, the community no longer accepted the fact that off-duty officers could use grill lights to pull over motorists. Particularly women motorists. To add to the pressure on HPD administrators to eliminate grill lights, several men in the community had blue grill lights installed in their vehicles specifically to impersonate police officers and pull over and harass motorists.

It didn't take long. No more grill lights. The police union fought the administration's decision on behalf of some of the officers who thought the brass went too far. But there would be no change of mind in this case. Too many women were being harassed on the roadways. In fact, the abolishment of grill lights was just a part of the new policy. A cop could still stop a vehicle while off duty, but he had to have a uniformed officer with a blue light on the roof of his car assist him. In fact, the administrators also suggested to motorists that if they were not sure if the vehicle trying to pull them over was a police officer, they could continue to drive, at a safe speed, to the nearest police station or substation.

This riled a lot of cops. It removed some of their authority. Some argued that drunk drivers continued to drive on, creating a danger for other motorists. Nevertheless, the new policy was here to stay, and the officers slowly became accustomed to the change.

Diane Suzuki's murder case included much more evidence, both direct and circumstantial, than did Lisa Au's.

On Saturday, July 6, 1985, at about three o'clock, Diane was seen speaking to a man near a two-tone Volkswagen with a lightning-like design on its side where the two paint colors met. After a little while, witnesses reported, Diane finished her conversation with the man and walked to the dance studio. The man walked in the opposite direction. This Volkswagen angle, however, stuck so much in the minds of a few investigators and prosecutors that they ignored the overwhelming direct and circumstantial evidence from the dance studio and pursued a phantom lead to apparent dead ends.

A few minutes after Diane's conversation with the man near the Volkswagen, another dance instructor saw Diane inside the studio, walking into the hallway that led to the bathroom of the second-floor dance studio. Another person who worked in the area was also present upstairs. According to the instructor, there was no one else in the dance studio. The instructor left and went downstairs. That was the last time anyone saw Diane Suzuki. But there was no evidence at that time to explain her disappearance.

A little later, three of Diane's friends arrived at the studio to meet her. The first to arrive went upstairs to look for her and was met by the person who was upstairs. He told her that Diane had left. The friend noticed that he had a cut on his finger. She also noticed that Diane's purse and bag were still there. The friend grabbed these and left.

Another friend went upstairs a few minutes after the first to look for Diane. She met the man, who said that he had not seen Diane, and who explained that he fell and cut himself with a pair of scissors.

A third friend went upstairs to look for Diane and was told by the man that he had not seen Diane.

Two days later, when detectives interviewed the man, he had scratches on his back, both arms, and left hand, and a cut on his left hand.

And Diane was not to be found.

The family had posters made, at least twenty thousand. Pictures of a smiling Diane wearing a necklace with a letter "D" pendant were placed all around Honolulu. Friends, neighbors, and family members got organized in a way that would have found someone who had just gone missing. Search after search was conducted. Diane's sister, Susan Suzuki, became the family spokesperson and patiently and tirelessly worked with police and the news media for years. The family and friends conscientiously did everything that people could do. They believed that no matter what had happened to Diane, they could find her and so they kept trying.

A few days later, detectives were sent to examine the dance studio. What they found was distressing. The bathroom door frame showed damage that indicated the door had been forced inward, breaking the jamb. Witnesses claimed that the door was not in that condition a few days earlier, and no one could explain how the door came to be damaged. Closer examination of the walls inside the bathroom, which were made of hollow tile, showed a dark substance inside the tiny depressions of the concrete. The police chemist stated that the specks were probably blood.

More spots were found on the floor of the bathroom. Test results showed they were indeed blood.

But no arrests followed. The evidence was not sufficient at that time.

Five years later, we had a new tool to take back to the crime scene and search for more evidence: luminol.

It did not take great effort to convince a judge that luminol, which was not available at the time of the initial investigation, could possibly show that a great amount of blood was spilled at one time in the studio bathroom where we believe Diane was murdered. With search warrant in hand, we returned to the studio, where we were greeted by the media. Apparently, someone from the police had advised the media that a search of the dance studio was about to take place.

The presence of the media, however, did not hamper our search, as they were not allowed inside the studio. It did mean that our return to the crime scene was now public knowledge. Our warrant asked the court to allow us to search for blood or the presence of blood using the new luminol technique. And we were not disappointed by our search. We were, however, initially challenged by some disappointing news: the floor of the bathroom had been replaced with new vinyl tile.

We had hoped that the floor would glow a bright blue, indicating the one-time presence of lots of blood. With the floor changed, we had to look at our task a little differently. How could we still conduct the test to see if someone had bled heavily in the bathroom? One officer had a good idea. Remove the new tile and see what was underneath.

We removed the tiles, darkened the room, and conducted the luminol test. What we found proved, at least in our minds, that there was a great quantity of blood on the floor of that bathroom at one time. A checkerboard outline covered nearly the entire floor in front of the toilet, and it glowed blue. What's the significance of that? The checkerboard outline represented the cracks between the old tiles that covered the floor. The blue glow was the positive luminol reaction. That meant that there once enough blood on the bathroom floor to cover the tiles and seep through the cracks between tiles to the concrete beneath. It also followed that the large quantity of blood was cleaned up by someone. And interestingly, the people who operated the dance studio and those who used it had no explanation for or memory of a large quantity of blood ever being spilled in the bath-room.

When we discussed this with a prosecutor who was tired of hear-ing us try to convince him that there was sufficient evidence to prose-cute, he dismissed us with a comment that the large number of women who used that bathroom could have carelessly spilled men-strual blood on the floor, giving us the luminol result. He could have just said "no." The menstrual blood comment was insulting. Let's see, a woman generally sheds an average of two fluid ounces of blood over five days of menstruation. So, the amount of blood that spilled on the bathroom floor would have taken some pretty serious effort by a lot of sloppy women. We later laughed over it. If that was the best that pros-ecutor could come up with, perhaps we actually did have hope that one day this circumstantial evidence would make it to a courtroom.

We completed the search of the dance studio five years after Diane Suzuki was reported missing. At the time of the search, some of the news media requested and received a look at court documents relating to Diane Suzuki's initial disappearance. Those 1985 records indicated that an initial interview with the man at the studio includ-ed a failed polygraph examination and a conclusion by detectives that he was "deceptive" when asked about her death. Although polygraph examinations are not admissible in court, police use them as a tool to help determine if those being questioned are telling the truth.

When we initially discussed preparing an affidavit for a warrant to search the studio, we also wanted to search the suspect's home. Prior to taking our request to the prosecutor and a judge for approval, we needed to clear this with our captain. He didn't believe that we had enough probable cause to search the suspect's home, and we couldn't convince him that we did. Our request was denied. This denial would prove to have interesting consequences.

About nine months after we searched the dance studio, we tried again and were successful in obtaining a search warrant for the sus-pect's property and surrounding areas. This time, we went with a large contingent of personnel. Detectives, SWAT (Specialized

Weapons and Tactics team), officers, army anthropologists, and members of the U.S. Army Central Identification Laboratory-Hawai'i (CILHI) were part of the search team. CILHI teams were experienced in searching Vietnam and other locations for remains of American military personnel. U.S. Army Sergeant Rick Huston coordinated the efforts for CILHI.

We met early in the day at Blaisdell Park in Pearl City—the same park that search teams had started from five years before—mobilized our units, and drove to the site of the search. Using the expert advice of the CILHI team, we assigned our personnel to conduct line and grid searches of the brush and swamp area to the rear of the suspect's home. Our teams searched the area for the entire day.

We did not find Diane Suzuki's body, but the day was not a total disappointment either. For reasons unknown, one officer decided to knock down the stump of an old banana tree he discovered. He dug around a little, and to everyone's surprise, found some clothing. This was exciting, because Diane Suzuki was described as wearing similar clothing on the day she disappeared. It was even more exciting because the sizes of the clothing were the right size for Diane.

Unfortunately, there was no way we could tie those articles of clothing to Diane Suzuki. They were degraded somewhat, and family members couldn't state for certain that they actually did belong to her. They would remain circumstantial evidence.

During the course of the search in the swamp, several officers noticed a difference in the colors of a rock retaining wall. Upon closer examination, they discovered that the darker brown rock appeared to be very old. The lighter-colored blue rock appeared to be much newer. The newer rock area rose from the ground about three feet and was about four feet wide. Everyone wanted to see what was behind that newer portion. The rocks were removed to reveal loosely packed dirt, along with twigs and leaves, that went in several feet deep. None of the vegetation should have been there if the wall was decades old, as was claimed by the suspect's family, who owned the house.

The army anthropologists took samples and reported back in a few weeks. In their opinion, the area was disturbed six to nine months before. We felt mixed emotions at that moment. Here was a site that by professional opinion was disturbed no more than nine months ago, at about the same time we searched the dance studio. It's all conjecture now on what we might have found had we been given approval to conduct the search when we initially wanted to. We believed we had found Diane Suzuki's gravesite.

Lisa Au's body was recovered, and her family was able to hold services and grieve together, and try to bring some feeling of closure to her senseless death. Diane Suzuki's family, as with the family of Marialyse Catell, never had that opportunity. They never got to be together with their beloved daughter and sister for one last time. And as long as our prosecutors hope for something or someone to come forward and give them the direct evidence they want, her family will never have the opportunity to possibly hear that one word that could add some sense of closure to their loss—*guilty*.

But all those posters of a smiling Diane Suzuki have kept her in *our* minds as well. The community remembers her, the smiling, pretty, approachable-looking girl next door.

Except she never came home.

Rest in peace, Diane.

17

The Insanity Defense to Murder

There is one element of the criminal justice system that drives people nuts—the insanity defense. To the layperson, the insanity defense lets killers get away with murder. It's horrifying to families of murder victims and to the community that people can kill and not be held responsible for their actions.

Our legal system defines the states of mind of people who commit crimes. The penal code breaks this concept into four degrees of intent. They are, in decreasing order of seriousness: intentional, knowing, reckless, and negligent. The criminal justice system also recognizes that there may be conditions under which a person's mental state will not fall into any of those categories. It recognizes that a person may be "insane" and not have the mental capacity to be responsible for his or her actions.

The term "insane" is a legal term, not a medical one. It means that when a person commits a crime, he or she could not tell right from wrong as a result of some medical mental illness or deficiency. The law holds that because of this, a person who is adjudicated insane at the time of the offense cannot be held responsible for his or her actions.

This concept is not new. It arose from English law in 1843. Daniel McNaughton believed that Prime Minister Sir Robert Peel was persecuting him. (Peel gained notoriety from his 1829 revisions to the London Metropolitan Police that introduced the concepts that the police are the community and the community is the police, that the police should consider public opinion in their actions, and that they should reduce their use of force in resolving conflict. The London Metropolitan Police nickname, "Bobby," came as a result of his reforms, which some people believe were the beginnings of community policing.) McNaughton, fearing what he saw as persecution by Peel, shot and killed Peel's secretary, believing the man to be Peel himself. The British court acquitted McNaughton of murder, ruling that McNaughton was not guilty by reason of insanity. He was placed into a mental institution, where he spent the rest of his life. The McNaughton Rule, as it came to be known, became a standard in both British and American law.

As with McNaughton, people acquitted due to "insanity" are not simply released back into the community. They are committed to a mental institution for treatment until physicians can successfully argue that they are cured and no longer a threat to other people in the community or a danger to themselves.

In recent years, however, some states have moved from the common "not guilty by reason of insanity" plea to a plea that accepts guilt, but with a reason due to mental illness. This change has come about because many juries have had great difficulty with the issue of the defendant's ability to understand right from wrong. This change in description of plea also clears the jury from the responsibility of deciding the accountability of a person who commits a crime while mentally ill.

Another claim that can be made by a defendant accused of a crime is "irresistible impulse." The person may argue that while he is capable of telling right from wrong, he was driven to commit the crime as a result of an internal irresistible impulse resulting from a mental illness. Interestingly, the same argument used by the defense—that the accused could not help himself, he acted impulsively—can be used by the prosecution. Even though we understand right from wrong, we all have impulses from time to time, but most people don't act on their impulses. If the accused understood right from wrong, he or she should be held accountable for his or her actions.

But what about the person who commits a crime—a murder, say—because he was drunk? Ever hear the expression "drunk no count"? That's local slang suggesting that you're not responsible for your actions if you're drunk. Nope. Hawai'i law states that if you're drunk, even dead skunk drunk, and you commit a criminal offense, you are just as responsible for your actions as if you were stone sober. Being intoxicated will not relieve you of your accountability for your actions and behavior. Not only are you accountable for your actions, if convicted you are subject to the same punishment that a sober defendant would receive—even if you have no memory of having committed the offense.

In an earlier chapter, we described how Lynn Kotis was murdered by her husband William Kotis. At his initial trial, Kotis was found by the court, as a result of psychiatric evaluation, to be unfit to stand trial. This is different from being found not guilty due to insanity. Essentially, the court said that, at the time of the trial, Kotis was mentally unfit to participate in his own defense. Ten years later, in 2002, psychiatrists found that Kotis's mental condition had improved. He was now fit to participate in his defense, and a trial date was set. A clinical psychologist found that Kotis's actions in 1992 when he murdered his wife were rational, and that Kotis was able to make the choice between right and wrong. Kotis was subsequently found guilty of the murder of Lynn Kotis and sentenced to life in prison.

A more recent case of someone found unfit to stand trial occurred on June 18, 2002. Retired *Honolulu Star Bulletin* sportswriter Jack Wyatt was walking along the Ala Wai Canal for his morning exercise. Witnesses said he was assaulted by forty-eight-year-old Cline Kahue, who pushed him into the canal. Wyatt apparently struck his head on some rocks, passed out, and drowned. Kahue continued walking on after attacking Wyatt and assaulted two women who were also walking along the canal, again as passersby watched. Police arrested Kahue, who tried to swim away from the crime scenes.

The year before, on March 8, 2001, Kahue was acquitted of four misdemeanor assault cases. He was found not guilty by reason of insanity. That he had previous acquittals of violent crimes due to insanity has raised many voices of concern. How could this man, with a history of violent behavior, be allowed back into society, where he could be a threat to other people only a year after having been judged insane? And obviously he was a fatal threat to Jack Wyatt. Did the system fail?

Like Kotis, Kahue was found unfit to stand trial for Wyatt's murder and was committed to the Hawai'i State Hospital for treatment. The odds are in Kahue's favor, however. If, like William Kotis, Kahue is ever found fit to stand trial for murder, he will have to prove that he was insane at the time of the killing. The prosecution will argue that he was sane. Kahue will probably use his mental illness as a defense. In this case, however, Kahue clearly showed that he understood that what he did was wrong. He tried to run away.

Still, if he is found to have been sane at the time of the killing, the circumstances point to a state of mind less than intentional. Kahue will likely argue that he didn't intend to cause the death of Wyatt. Rather, his actions were reckless—that by pushing Wyatt into the canal, he risked a danger that Wyatt could have been injured sufficiently to have caused Wyatt's death.

In either case, it appears that Kahue may have sufficient legal precedent to technically get away with murder.

18
The Murder of Garrick Lee

While we knew that blood spatter can help police reconstruct a crime scene, we learned during the murder investigation of Roland Kotani just how accurately that blood spatter can describe the actual sequence of events during a crime. But even though blood spatter can be a helpful tool, it can also create confusion. The murder of Garrick Lee was one of those cases in which blood told a confusing story—one that left us puzzled.

In January 1990, Garrick Lee, thirty-four, of Nu'uanu, was an employee of Kamaaina Metals, located near Ala Moana Center. On January 12, he and a group of coworkers went out after work for dinner and drinks. Investigators learned later that after the merry-making, Lee drove a woman coworker back to their shop's parking lot, where she had left her car.

At about 1:15 A.M. on January 13, a security guard walking through the warehouses at what was then the 404 Pi'ikoi complex heard a gunshot. One gunshot. The guard turned in the direction of the blast and saw a man run from the parking lot, turn onto Pi'ikoi Street, and disappear into the dark.

In the parking lot from which the man ran was a car. It was facing headfirst into its stall. Lee was in the driver's seat, slumped onto the passenger side. He had been shot in the head and was dead at the scene. A small pool of blood collected at his head, which was resting on the passenger seat. More blood flowed under the seat's backrest and dripped to the right rear passenger floor, staining the carpet a dark red. His injury was a through-and-through bullet wound that entered the midleft side of his head and exited the midright side.

The vehicle was a gray Mercedes sedan. The front passenger door was ajar, and all the windows were down.

The Homicide Detail arrived just a few minutes before it started to rain. Not a heavy, pouring rain, but a steady drizzle. Standing with the patrol officers was a woman. She confirmed that she and a group of coworkers had gone out earlier that night for dinner and some drinks.

She also told investigators that Lee had driven her back to the parking lot to get her car. She was sitting in the front passenger seat of Lee's car, and when he parked, she got out and stood momentarily at the open passenger door, saying good night to him. Suddenly, there was an explosion and a bright flash. He fell sideways onto the passenger seat and there was blood coming from his head. The woman told investigators that she screamed. She didn't see the person who shot Lee, but saw the flash from the gun.

In spite of the physical evidence that initially seemed to corroborate the woman's statement, investigators suspected the woman was not telling the entire truth. And one abnormality in the blood spatter pattern confused and frustrated us.

It's not difficult to understand blood spatter. Think about the times you've cut your finger and drops of blood have fallen to the ground or onto a counter. This field of study even has a name: bloodstain pattern analysis. The term "blood spatter," however, is a whole lot easier to say. Blood spatter comes in different forms, each representing a different pattern or shape. The differences can also represent the manner in which the blood was ejected from the body.

Perhaps the most frequently seen type of blood spatter is the *blood droplet* in the shape of a teardrop. Whether this teardrop-shaped blood droplet is slightly round or elongated depends on the angle at which it strikes the surface that it lands on. The point of the teardrop indicates the direction it was traveling at time of impact. An elongated drop may also have little splotches called "satellites" just past the point of the teardrop. When the blood droplet is round or nearly round, it usually indicates that the blood fell at a 90-degree angle to the surface.

Crime scene analysts can, with the proper equipment, use a template to measure the angle at which the blood droplet hit the surface. By attaching a string to the point of the droplet and bringing this string away from the surface at the prescribed angle, they can determine the exact spot in space—at the convergence point of the string with other strings—where the injury that caused the blood spatter occurred. That this can be done is a credit to the scientist who developed the formula. That some evidence specialists actually do it is an indication that they have way too much time on their hands. In the vast majority of cases, there is little reason to actually determine where the blood spatter originated. It is enough to know that it occurred.

Blood spatter analysis plays a large role in reconstruction at bloody scenes. Blood spatter can indicate where the blood came from or perhaps the movement of the victim to different locations. The position of the body provides a point from which to work backward. Using all the information available allows the investigator to piece together a story of what happened.

Arterial blood spatter occurs when a large vein or artery is cut and clumps of blood are ejected from this wound onto a surface. When this occurs, we usually see the stain created when the blood struck the wall, then the line of blood that flowed or rolled down the wall from the initial clump of blood. Each of these clumps of arterial blood spatter represents the beat of a heart as each pump pushed the blood from the wound.

An example of arterial blood spatter analysis comes from the murder scene of a young woman who was stabbed to death on September 1, 1983, near the University of Hawai'i. Patricia Marks, 23, decided to remain in her apartment while her boyfriend went upstairs to a friend's apartment to play cards. A few hours later, she called him on the telephone and told him that someone was breaking in through the kitchen window. He told her it was her imagination and that she should go back to sleep. Several hours later, he returned to the apartment and found her lying on the living-room floor naked, bound and gagged, and stabbed to death. She had also been sexually assaulted.

Arterial blood spatter on the wall next to her body appeared in regular four-inch intervals; then there was no blood on the wall for about two feet; then there was more arterial blood spatter in a similar pattern. A logical explanation for the area on the wall without the arterial blood spatter is that the suspect was straddling her when he inflicted the wound. The blood that would have stained the wall struck him instead. That alerted officers that the suspect's clothing or body would likely be bloody. Unfortunately, Patricia Marks' murder was never solved.

High-velocity blood spatter occurs when the wound is made by a means involving great force, such as a gunshot. High-velocity blood spatter is composed of a multitude of tiny spots of blood, similar to the mist of saliva that occurs in an unprotected sneeze. High-velocity blood spatter can occur from the entrance wound of a gunshot and again from the exit wound.

Cast-off blood spatter occurs when blood accumulates on an instrument or weapon and flies off when the weapon or instrument is jerked back from the wound. This is usually seen as random, formless clumps of blood on a wall or surface opposite the injury. However, the motion of the assailant's arm or weapon will affect the location of the cast-off blood spatter. We saw this occur in the Roland Kotani murder.

A little bit of physics comes into play when describing blood spatter. Spatter will fly in a straight line until interrupted by an object or until gravity pulls it downward. In that regard, the blood spatter in

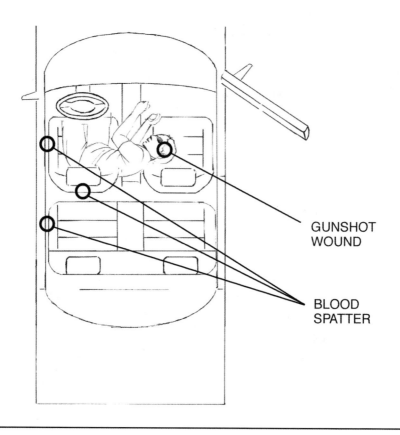

The blood spatter pattern in Garrick Lee's vehicle

Lee's car didn't make any sense. We found high-velocity blood spatter on the upper portion of the inside panel of the driver's front door. This would be normal and expected in a close-range gunshot wound to the head. There would be some high-velocity blood spatter coming back toward the shooter. This is called *blow back*, and explains why in some murder cases the victim's blood can be found inside the barrel of the murder weapon.

But when we examined the car closely, we found similar high-velocity blood spatter to the middle-upper portion of the inside panel of the driver's side *rear* passenger seat. How could that be? The driver was shot as he sat in the front seat.

But wait. We also found high-velocity blood spatter on the back of the driver's seat. His companion told us the driver was shot on the other side of the seat in the side of his head from outside the driver's door. How could the blood get to the back of his seat?

Something was very wrong here. Was the woman lying? The blood spatter was in three different locations, two of which simple physics made impossible.

Investigators processed Lee's car and interviewed his friends and family. We didn't come up with anything of major value in our processing of the car, but we learned some interesting information from our interviews. Some of the witnesses suggested that the victim was involved in drugs, and perhaps didn't pay his drug bills, and was killed as an example to others to pay their drug debts.

But investigators were still stumped as to the reconstruction of the killing. Some of their questions remain unanswered:

• What happened to the bullet?
    We found no evidence of the bullet impacting anywhere inside the vehicle and no evidence of the bullet or its fragments outside the car.

• Was there blood outside the vehicle?
    We didn't find any, but that's not to say there wasn't some blood there prior to our arrival. Remember, it was raining.

• Could there have been suspects in addition to the man who ran away?
    Not likely. The security guard saw only one person leave, and the woman remained there, waiting for the police to arrive.

• Was a weapon recovered?
    Yes. A weapon was recovered from a planter box on Pi'ikoi Street. Its caliber matched the size of the injury on the victim's head.

• Did all the blood belong to the victim?

> Yes, as far as we could tell. The ABO blood-typing analysis of the blood showed a match in all locations to the victim's own blood type.

We suspected that the woman was lying. Because of the placement of Lee's injury, her statement that she was standing just outside the car at the passenger door saying goodnight to the victim when he was shot could not be true. He was shot on the midleft side of his head and the bullet exited on the midright side of his head. Had he been looking at her and saying goodnight as she claimed, his entry wound would have been closer to the left-rear of his head, and his exit wound would have been to his right temple.

If her statement was true, the shooter would have had to fire the weapon with the bullet passing through the windshield. The windshield was not broken.

We know that blood spatter, like everything else, will fly in a straight line until gravity brings it down—or until it lands on something. In cases like this, the impact of the bullet on a victim's head occurs with such great force that high-velocity blood spatter sprays from both the entry wound and the exit wound.

So if we believe that all the blood came from the one wound created by the one gunshot, it would not be possible for the blood to get on the three separate surfaces.

And how that happened remains a mystery.

19
George Fan—Murder or Suicide?

On June 22, 1990, the body of developer George Fan was found near a palm tree in Makiki District Park, not far from his home. He was neatly gagged, and his wallet and wristwatch were missing. In the pocket where his wallet should have been was a nearly spent roll of masking tape, apparently the same roll of tape used to gag him. Police opened a homicide investigation.

Fan's wife told investigators that he had left the night before. His car was found in its parking stall, but that wasn't unusual. He sometimes went for nighttime walks. His wife also said that it was his habit to carry cash, sometimes several hundred dollars, because he didn't like to be without money.

In August, toxicology results showed that Fan had diazepam (also known as Valium), codeine, morphine, and diphenhydramine, an antihistamine, in his blood. Chief Medical Examiner Alvin Omori reported that Fan committed suicide.

Police disagreed. Fan had abrasions to his nose and forehead that were observed by police investigators at the scene. Surprisingly, Dr. Omori's staff reported to the media that Fan had no visible injuries. And he was carefully gagged with the masking tape, with each wrap of the tape falling neatly on top of the earlier wraps. If he did gag himself, how could he have done such neat work without seeing what he was doing? Why would he have the presence of mind to be that careful if he was so distraught that he was plotting to end his own life? If he was so certain that he would kill himself by way of a drug overdose, why would he bother gagging himself?

Investigators had questions not easily answered by the medical examiner's conclusion of suicide as a manner of death.

• Many people saw the minor abrasions to Fan's face. Why did the medical examiner's office report that Fan had no visible injuries?

• What happened to Fan's wallet and wristwatch? An extensive search was conducted of Makiki District Park and neither was found.

• If Fan indeed committed suicide, did he have an accomplice?

• Did the medical examiner develop a motive for suicide? From the perspective of investigators, there was a motive for murder: robbery.

The investigation into Fan's death took many turns. Fan, a previous president of the Hawaiian Chinese Civic Association, had financial troubles at the time of his death. His development company, GNP Development Ventures, defaulted on the construction loan for the Country Club Plaza condominium in Salt Lake in 1985. His financial troubles were mounting. Could there be a connection between that and his death? It was known that he gambled, and some investigators wondered if there was a connection there. Fan had other problems. In April of 1989, he was arrested for threatening a former business partner. Fan allegedly walked into the man's Fort Street Mall office carrying a golf bag, from which he pulled a loaded shotgun. He was charged with first-degree terroristic threatening and a firearms offense. At a preliminary hearing, Fan asked the court for a trial delay so he could raise money to hire an attorney for his defense. But he never got his day in court. Did all that add up to a pronouncement of suicide ?

An August 17, 1990, *Honolulu Advertiser* article reported Frank Quallen, the chief investigator for the medical examiner's office, as saying that Fan's overdose was self-administered. How did they know that? Could it not have been possible that Fan was forced to take an overdose of drugs? Police investigators who worked the Makiki District Park crime scene thought that Fan's death was a murder.

How did *they* know *that*? Neither the medical examiner's personnel nor the police were present at the time that the drugs entered George Fan's body. Nor were they there when he died. Yet both made quick conclusions.

It seems apparent that the toxicology evidence of the drug overdose was sufficient for Dr. Alvin Omori to conclude that Fan killed himself. On the other hand, others have asked, could the drugs have been administered by someone other than Fan himself? Could Fan have been robbed of his watch and wallet? Could the minor injuries to his face have been caused by his being pushed up against the concrete wall of the park's restroom?

Was George Fan murdered?

Or did he commit suicide, as concluded by Dr. Omori?

We don't know. That's the key. We weren't there. That's the issue. And not having that knowledge is the powerful motivating force behind continuing to investigate suspicious deaths as homicides. We have an obligation—to our community, to George Fan, to his family—to investigate his death to the investigation's utmost end. To leave no clue or lead incomplete. To make no premature conclusion.

The differences in opinion regarding the manner of George Fan's death highlight an area of criminal justice and the law that some people don't agree with. The Office of the Medical Examiner is responsible for determining not only the medical cause of death, but also the manner of death.

The medical cause of death can be anything . . . a heart attack, cancer, stroke. The manner of death, on the other hand, is very limited. It will be either a natural death, whether attended by a physician or not; an accident, regardless of what kind of accident; a suicide; or a homicide. Murder, manslaughter, and negligent homicide all fall under the category of homicide.

For one person to have the sole authority to make a judgment on medical cause of death *and* legal manner of death is a precarious situation that can lead to problems if that person has a difference of opinion with investigators or prosecutors. If investigative efforts show that a person committed homicide, but the autopsy results show that the victim's manner of death was something else, such as natural, accidental, or suicide, it's very difficult to bring charges of murder or manslaughter.

Under such circumstances, prosecutors must bring in an outside second opinion if they want to pursue charges that contradict the original pathologist's conclusion. And if that second opinion contradicts the original opinion of the pathologist who performed the autopsy, interagency conflict and disagreement can result. If the outside opinion is accepted in court, it embarrasses the pathologist who made the original call. Prosecutors want to avoid situations like this. They must work with the local pathologist on other cases and don't want to have a poor relationship with him or her.

George Fan may indeed have committed suicide. But at the time of the investigation into his death, Dr. Alvin Omori had another option available to him. If he did not agree that Fan was a victim of homicide, he could have deferred his conclusion on the manner of death by declaring it "undetermined" while homicide investigators continued to search for the answers to their nagging questions. It would have offered the police an opportunity to further their exploration into the case. It would have offered the medical examiner's office an opportunity to possibly obtain more confirmation on the circumstances of Fan's death. Because once the conclusion of suicide is applied to a death, the intensity of the homicide investigation will undoubtedly come to an end. The urgency to locate witnesses or uncover evidence or leads or suspects ends there, perhaps prematurely.

Remember the concepts *organization, thoroughness,* and *caution* we mentioned in the Introduction? In every death investigation, we need to be as organized, as thorough, and as cautious as possible in our investigative efforts.

We simply cannot do less.

From a Reporter's Perspective

Reporters and cops just don't see things the same; never have, probably never will. Each pretty much considers the other one of the irritating realities of their professional lives. And some conflicts are inevitable.

Reporters are trying to get information and then tell everyone they can about what they find. Most are under pressure from their bosses to get information quickly, get more, and get it before any other reporters can beat them to it.

Police use information as a different kind of commodity. Specific, detailed information about a case is closely guarded by investigators because it can lead conclusively to a suspect in a crime. If everyone knows the information, it is harder to sift out who is telling the truth from those who are just trying to get attention. It is harder to prove conclusively that they've found the right suspect when key details are widely known. Reporters look at the same information as important for their work, interesting details that tell the story better for readers or viewers.

Still, the two professions really do need each other. (The public doesn't trust either of us all that much.) Police depend on the news media to get the word out: to help spread the word about crimes, to publicize sketches of suspects, to warn people of consumer scams in the community. People are interested in police news and want to hear about murders, stupid criminals like the bank robber who writes his demand note on his deposit slip, and even the average police-blotter news about a burglary of a house down the street. All those stories affect the community. If the house near your mother was broken into during the day, you want to remind her about locking up. Generally, most of us care about what happens to our neighbors. We do still live in that small town that just happens to have grown pretty big.

The police–news media relationship works best when both sides realize that they need each other and that each has an important function. Many crimes have been solved faster because publicity put out by the news media—the missing man's description in the newspaper, the radio broadcast of a license number and direction of a suspect, the televised image of the bank robber—brought tips and clues. When the police-media relationship remains completely adversarial, it often fails.

So, with all this distrust going on, how can police and the media ever reach a workable relationship? It starts with each side recognizing the value of the other's role, including knowing what the other is seeking. It continues to work when both sides see that it can work. Police can start with the basic five "w's" of reporting: who, what, when, where, why—and then throw in the how. Officials don't have to tell reporters all they know, but they do need to give a basic account of crimes that occur in the community. Reporters can help by telling the police what they need to know. Police shouldn't be expected to watch every newscast and read every newspaper, but they should pay attention to news stories.

Generally, folks who work in the news media diligently work to be objective, fair, and accurate. Some fall short; they ask shallow questions, show their own views in their stories, and play favorites. Some police officers from various ranks helpfully provide information to reporters as long as they are not named. That practice frustrates investigators assigned to individual cases; they become protective of any information that may be crucial to resolving the cases. But when a law enforcement agency stifles one source of information, it will usually see the information seep out in other places. Some officials would be very surprised to learn which of their colleagues provide information to the news media. Sure, some are cases of people who just like the attention or have a personal agenda. But most place the information in the hands of reporters they have developed some trust in so that news will emerge on significant stories or developments.

And most reporters who cover a beat develop a respect for those they encounter. That's true even though reporters and police are often cynical or hardened by some of the bad things they see.

As much as reporters in Honolulu still complain about the lack of consistent information from the police department here and in the other counties, it has been worse. In the 1980s, many police officers seemed proud of how little they would say to reporters and how difficult they would make it for reporters to get basic information. In turn, reporters got pretty crafty about finding information, and some police officials would talk about cases, but on the condition that they not be named. By the time the 1990s rolled around and Police Chief Mike Nakamura took over, he recognized that police-media relations could use some improvement. That's not to say that no other police officers treated reporters fairly before Nakamura. Some did, but institutionally, the Honolulu Police Department was very protective of information.

For most police news, reporters often relied on unnamed sources to flesh out the details. Stories would say: "Police said the two men and a woman were suspects in the robbery-murder" or "Detectives said the killer is suspected to be someone who turned on the victim, with evidence of the special animosity often found in a hate crime, where the victim is targeted for his or her gender, race or sexual orientation." That worked okay for some cases but seemed ludicrous in others. For a short story about a bank robbery in which no one was injured or an account of a traffic fatality, the references to officials seem acceptable. But crank up the intensity to cases that involve schools, children, multiple victims, crime in places where people expect they are usually safe, and a host of crimes, and those unnamed officials start to seem mighty suspicious. Questions pop up. Why won't they talk on the record about their investigation? What are they hiding? What are they afraid of? Confidence wanes that the right people are doing the right thing for the right reason. Justice shouldn't be sneaky.

One summer evening in 1982 (before Nakamura), a couple of people burst into a ballroom dancing class in the McCully area and robbed the class members of money and jewelry. Reporters got there nearly as fast as police. One of the detectives had allowed members of the public to come in and talk with people who had been robbed. Then he noticed that reporters and photographers were gathered outside the door where the victims were waiting and talking. So, even though we were politely standing outside waiting for the police to finish their initial interviews, this detective shot us a dirty look and slammed the cafeteria door. He could have done it differently but saw no need to and probably felt few qualms about it at the time.

The reporters complained about it, even to some of the other detectives. Those detectives agreed that the officer was sometimes an obnoxious jerk, but even the enlightened ones weren't all that alarmed by his actions. Was he protecting the case? Well, then, okay, that was a lousy way to do it, but . . .

That kind of action often causes a reaction. What about the next time that detective meets the same news media folks? What if he slips and falls while on his way into or out of the crime scene? What if he says something that makes him sound foolish? What if he asks for special consideration—take a certain photo, highlight an aspect of a witness statement, or hold back on something because it's sensitive to the investigation? Odds are, he's not going to get a lot of sympathy or help. Is that mean or less than professionally objective? Sure, but so was he, and news media types are people too. Really.

Leave all the news media standing in the sun for hours without giving them basic information and they'll work hard to find information themselves. They'll interview witnesses before the police can find them. They'll ask the neighbors questions and get themselves invited into their homes; they'll climb on their roofs or out their windows to get a better look at whatever the police are trying to hide.

An investigator who treats people fairly often gets back the same kind of consideration. Provide the basic information in a timely manner and reporters and photographers will often supply helpful information: "You guys wanna talk to that man over there. He just got home but said that he talked to the victims yesterday." "Some kids a block away found a gun in the dumpster." "The landlady said the people next door just paid cash for a new truck."

Reporters can also steer police away from misleading information provided by people at the scene. Sometimes helpful neighbors provide crucial information about what they saw and heard. But sometimes they just want to be on TV or in the newspaper. At one murder in Waikīkī, a man was killed in his apartment in the Gold Coast area of pricey apartments near Diamond Head. Helpful and seemingly sincere neighbors came out and shook their heads over the tragedy, then offered their observations about what time they heard the gunshots. Only trouble is, the victim was stabbed to death. Teenagers and elderly folks are most often guilty of embellishing their memories to get on TV or to be quoted in the newspaper. That's why it's important for reporters to take the time at the scene to do a mini-investigation—to talk to several people, to check with investigators, to trust our instincts about what alleys to avoid and what people to doubt.

(As shorthand, when we talk about news media or reporters, we're lumping in photographers, both still and video, as the people on the scene doing the news-gathering. In this day of more media companies working to cover more news with fewer people or to respond to formula news themes, photographers sometimes spend more time at scenes than the reporters and they often have longer institutional memories of the events in the community.)

The news media and the police spend a lot of time waiting around. When reporters stake out a crime scene awaiting an official interview, often hours of waiting are punctuated by minutes of frantic activity as the news media try to pry bits of information out of officials. Sometimes the hours drag by, with both sides tolerating one another. Other times, the police and the reporters get to know each other better while developing a better long-term understanding. Other times they just get crabbier and more ornery.

Some situations often combine tedium and danger. While most people instinctively run *away* from the sounds of gunshots, disasters, and other alarms, the news media as well as the cops run *toward* the sound of danger. The news media try to keep out of the way of emergency workers and follow basic precautions. But in an area where shots have been threatened or fired, tempers fray, and sometimes officials try to push the news media so far away that they can't know what's happening. They may do it under the pretext of ensuring that the news media remain out of danger, but it's an abuse of power.

Some officials assess situations and gauge risks in a way that everyone can accept. Others show their grace and basic kindness even in stressful situations. One hostage standoff in Waipahu drew police, news media, and curious members of the community from all over the island because the men being sought were suspects in at least one murder. The report of their discovery emerged in the afternoon, but the standoff continued for hours, leaving the news media scouring the neighborhood for information for hours after dark. Among the many officials present were motorcycle patrol officers helping with traffic control. Officer Roy Thurman, who later died in a traffic collision while working in rush hour, was on the scene. He got his job done, keeping folks back from the line of fire, but also chatted politely with reporters about his wife and young daughter. When he noticed late in the evening that I didn't have a jacket on that cool night, he found a spare jacket of his own and lent it to me in a kind, brotherly way. By the following day, in warmer weather, I tracked him down, threw a sweater of my own in the news car, and returned the jacket. His small gesture made a big impression about the difference that just one person can make in creating the public's image of how police act. He came across like the beat cop in children's books, someone you could turn to for help, and not a cop interested only in handing out a lot of traffic tickets.

The police-media relationship is a work in progress. It gets better, it gets worse. Other states and cities seem far more committed to making it work. Many here in Hawai'i fall back on the old ways if they aren't encouraged by their leadership to remember their public role.

Many government agencies, including the police, handle media relations in a businesslike manner, with personnel who specialize in dealing with the media. Reporters know where to go, and the agency gets the word out on routine news more accurately, effectively, and efficiently. When the news media need or want more information from the police, they can go to the detectives, officers, or specialists handling the cases they are pursuing. There are some drawbacks to that system, since it gives others in the police department an appointed spokesperson to hide behind. It is often better to talk with those closer to the case to get the best understanding. But having someone designated to handle the basic news helps simplify the day for police—who don't have to keep fielding the same question over and over—and for reporters who can get the bottom-line police news quickly.

A big challenge for reporters in the field, especially at crime scenes, is those wanna-be witnesses like the folks in Waikīkī who wanted to have heard gunshots, even though their neighbor died of stab wounds. Those "witnesses" are otherwise helpful people. Really helpful. They sometimes listen to what others around them say, and nod, adding only minor details. Often teenagers in groups will volunteer information, sometimes mischievously; other times they will just search their memories for anything relevant.

Reporters and photographers need to observe the people they speak with, check facts, and use some judgment about what "witness" statements should be part of the news.

Reporters are happiest talking to people out in the field, because that gives them a chance to walk in the shoes of those they are writing about, or at least to experience some of what they see and do. It helps make every day different and it helps to encourage and discourage them on different days about human nature. Writing the story can be another big draw to the profession: the excitement of finding the right words, the thrill of having a story that no one else has. But ask most reporters what drew them to the job and they will talk more about gathering the news than writing it: the chance to piece together a complex crime as the detectives do, learn how a fire investigator can tell a house fire was arson from the burn pattern on the wall, watch a paramedic bring someone back from the brink of death.

Veteran *Honolulu Star-Bulletin* reporter Phil Mayer, who started his career at the *New York Times,* showed his keen insight when he said he believes that most reporters are essentially very shy but very curious people. Our jobs give us the excuse to ask all those questions we're wondering about anyway.

The job of a reporter also takes us into the community, seeing people at their best and at their worst. We often cover events: the graduations, the awards, the murders, the failures. Then we move on to the next story.

This book provided a rare opportunity to look at some of Honolulu's best-known murders from the perspective of both the insider lead detective and the veteran reporter pressing for some of the same answers from the outside.

We think the cooperation results in a behind-the-scenes look that provides insight into the crimes and the people so deeply affected by them. Working together gave us the chance to add a dimension to the accounts that would not have been possible without the unusual collaboration. Writing the book brought its own challenges, going back through some very painful times for those involved. And some of the same tension arose, the continuing seesaw between the reporter's drive to tell the compelling stories and the detective's need to protect the case, to never give up the hope that each homicide will be solved.

Postscript

Remember the concept of *kīnā'ole*?

> *Do the right thing, in the right way, at the right time,*
> *in the right place, to the right person, for the right reason,*
> *with the right feeling . . . the first time.*

Too often, we have only the first time to be organized, and thorough, and cautious. In death investigations, when we close our minds to other perspectives and possibilities and prematurely come to what may appear to be the obvious conclusion, we may do great injustice to the dead.

Another underlying principle is the sacredness of life. All life has value. And all human life has equal value. There should be no distinction between the murder of a state representative and that of a downtown drunk. We must never lose sight of the intense, emotional, and catastrophic loss that occurs in a homicide.

Goethe once said, *Things which matter most must never be at the mercy of things which matter least.* The investigation into the murder of a human being is something that matters most. Overtime, a football game, or even a quick conclusion to an incomplete investigation—these are the things that matter least. And these are the things that must never corrupt the homicide investigation.

Organization, thoroughness, caution, and the concept of *kīnā'ole* apply not only to police homicide investigators. Police administrators, prosecutors, judges, defense attorneys, parole and probation officers, medical examiners—all the members of the criminal justice system—have an obligation to the victim to be sure that they have thoroughly completed their investigative efforts to the best of their ability.

The first time.